Girl, Let Go: Ditching Toxic Love

I0527920

Your Power Path to Self-Discovery, Healing, and Thriving After Emotional Abuse

Preface

"You can't let your mistakes define your day, let alone your life.

Flip the script and make lemonade out of those lemons, honey!" - An Unlikely Wise Man

Welcome to Your Transformation Journey

Visualize yourself sipping on that sweet, tangy lemonade made from the lemons life handed you, savoring the triumph of turning a sour situation into something delightful. That's what we're about to do together in these pages. We're flipping scripts and reclaiming narratives. This isn't just a book; it's a roadmap, a confidante, and a cheerleader rolled into one, guiding you out of the shadows of toxic relationships and into the sunlight of self-worth and freedom.

You might be feeling stuck, honey, weighed down by a love that's got more conditions than an iTunes agreement. It's that sneaky kind of love, sugar-coated with sweet nothings, only to leave you feeling less than nothing. I've been there, watched dear friends navigate those choppy waters, and honey, it's a ride nobody deserves a ticket for.

Why I Wrote This Book

I was inspired to write this book because, at its core, it's about liberation – and not just from that no-good partner who can't appreciate the phenomenal person you are. It's about breaking free from the mental chains of "what ifs" and "if onlys" that hold us back from recognizing our true worth. It's about realizing that the only validation we ever need is from the person staring back at us in the mirror.

Now, why me, you ask? Well, after gong through my own healing from a terrible relationship, I've continued to see friends and family members stuck in this cycle, walking on eggshells around partners who wouldn't know a healthy relationship if it came with a user manual. I've been the shoulder to cry on, the 3 AM call, and the "girl, let me tell you" storyteller. It broke my heart because I've been there, but it also fired me up to spread the word: enough is enough.

Shout Outs and Hugs

Big love and the warmest of hugs to the true champions in my life. A special shout out to my mom and Auntie Pat - you're both my rocks and guiding stars, shining bright with wisdom and unconditional love. To the incredible experts who enlightened us with their profound insights, you're not just brainy – you've got heart and soul in every word. And to you, my reader, for trusting me with your time and spirit, for bringing your heart to these pages and sharing this journey with me. You're not just a reader; you're an essential part of this story, the real MVP. Let's keep turning these pages together, growing and healing in unity.

For Whom This Book Sings

If you've ever caught yourself thinking, "Is it me?" after a partner served you cold indifference or piping hot criticism, this is your anthem. If you dread nights alone because the silence speaks louder than any harsh word, pull up a chair. This book sings for the broken-hearted who still dare to dream of love, but more importantly, it's a ballad for those ready to fall head over heels for themselves.

Listen, I'm not promising a fairy tale ending, but I am promising the start of something beautiful – a journey back to you. Expect revelations, aha moments, and yes, a healthy serving of sass. I'll guide you through recognizing those toxic tango steps, building your self-esteem fortress, and strutting out of that emotional maze like the royalty you are.

Take My Hand, Let's Leap

Thank you for investing your hope and heart in these words. Whether you're tucked away in a cozy nook of your home, or finding a moment of peace in a hectic day, know this: you're not alone. So, take a deep breath, turn the page, and let's step into your new chapter, where you're the writer, the director, and yes, the star of your story.

Ready to turn those lemons into lemonade? Come on,sis, let's do this thing.

Chapter 1: Beyond the Fog: Recognizing Toxic Love

Lena's feet carried her along the sun-dappled sidewalk of Front St, in the late afternoon sun casting long, lazy shadows that stretched like cats in the warmth. The air, thick with the fragrance of nearing summer, hugged her skin as she walked, a procession of thoughts just as heavy on her mind.

It was a normal Thursday, but the weight of the ring on her finger felt heavier than the humid air, a symbol of love entangled with chains of manipulation. She passed the familiar bookstore, where once she and Marcus had spent hours losing themselves in tales of romance and adventure, it now stood as a silent witness to the blurry lines of their own story.

Inside her, a battle waged quiet but fierce. Marcus had a silver tongue that could weave guilt and affection into the same sentence, his "I love yous" peppered with reminders of her supposed flaws. She thought of her mama, a woman whose spine was set strong like the ancient oaks of Crescent Avenue; she wouldn't have let no man dim her shine.

Lena recalled the way Marcus would apologize, his touch soft as the petal of a rose, that would later turn to thorns. Her empathetic heart tried to rationalize, to see the hurt child within him, but these days, she found herself questioning whether his sob stories were just another way to keep her tethered.

Shifting her sight to the children playing in the park, laughter dancing on the breeze, she glimpsed what joy unchecked looked like. What if she sought that freedom? The thought bloomed in her chest like the roses in front of the old library—unfettered and reaching for the sun.

With each block, the conversation with her sister friend echoed, who had told her, "Girl, you gotta be brave enough to choose you, always." But bravery was a tall order when a heart was involved, wasn't it?

As the sky began to tuck the sun into bed, hues of orange and purple painting the horizon of her beloved city, Lena felt a newfound courage whisper from the depths. She could almost hear her future self, full of sass and resilience, urging her to cut ties that bound, not support.

"Honey, when did loving someone mean losing you?" the voice seemed to ask.

She paused at the corner of a bustling street, sounds of life and living vibrating through the air, a question hanging on her lips as if the evening itself leaned in to listen. Wasn't the bravest act of love, after all, the love you gave yourself?

Lena stood there, at the crossroads, not just of Front St, but of her life. The question resonated within her like a church bell on Sunday morning. Wasn't it true? Loving someone shouldn't come with the cost of losing oneself. Yet, here she was, a living testament to that sacrifice.

The night air wrapped around her like a promise as she took a deep breath. The city lights twinkled like stars fallen to earth, each one a story, a struggle, a triumph. Lena's mind wandered to the tales her grandmother used to tell her - stories of women warriors, queens of their own destinies. They didn't wear capes; their strength was in their resilience, their power in their choices. It was time, she realized, to author her own story.

Walking past the café where she and Marcus had shared countless cups of coffee, discussing dreams that seemed to have faded like the old wallpaper, Lena felt a stirring. Dreams didn't die; they were just buried under layers of doubt and fear. Hers were still there, waiting to be reignited.

She recalled her early yoga classes, where she learned the power of breath and intention. Breathing in, she imagined drawing in strength and clarity; breathing out, she released confusion and hurt. With each step, Lena felt a little more of her old self returning, the part that laughed freely and dreamt boldly.

Her phone buzzed, breaking her reverie. It was Marcus, with his usual "Where are you?" text. Once, those words would have sent her rushing back, her heart tangled in a web of guilt and obligation. But tonight, the words seemed small, almost insignificant against the backdrop of her awakening.

Lena typed a response, her fingers steady. "Taking some time for myself. We need to talk when I get back." She hit send before she could second guess herself. This was more than a text; it was a declaration, a first step in setting boundaries, in choosing herself.

As she continued her walk, Lena felt an unexpected sense of peace. She wasn't sure what tomorrow would bring, or how the conversation with Marcus would go. But she knew one thing for sure: she was no longer content being a passenger in her own life. It was time to take the wheel.

In the soft embrace of the night, Lena whispered a promise to herself, a vow of self-love and respect. She wouldn't have all the answers by dawn, but she had the most important one: she was worth fighting for.

When Love Feels Like a Battlefield

Let's dive right into it, shall we? Picture this: you're standing in the thick of what feels like an emotional fog, unable to see clearly, feeling every bit of warmth and affection yet stinging from the cuts of words and actions that don't match up. Welcome to the tricky territories of toxic love, where the lines between affection and manipulation blur as if someone smeared Vaseline on your glasses. In this journey, we're about to unravel this complex tapestry, stitch by stitch.

You may be nodding along, recognizing this fog all too well. After all, for those of us with hearts as wide as the New Jersey Turnpike, distinguishing love from manipulation isn't as straightforward as we wish it were. It's like trying to tell the difference between a genuine "I'm sorry" and one that's just trying to get you to lower your guard. And let me tell you, that's a fine line thinner than a hair strand at times.

For the empathetic souls among us, this chapter is your

flashlight in the fog. We're not just identifying the neon signs of toxic love; we're understanding why our big, beautiful hearts can sometimes lead us astray. You see, us empath types, we've got a habit of seeing the potential, the 'could-be's, over the blatant 'what-is.' We make excuses, rationalize, and often end up carrying the emotional load of a relationship that's supposed to be a two-way street.

But here's the kicker—*cultivating the courage to prioritize our well-being isn't about turning our backs on love.* It's about recognizing when love is serving us whole wheat, nutritional goodness, and when it's dishing out empty calories that leave us more malnourished the more we consume. Recognizing this difference is your ticket out of the fog and into the sunlight.

In the narratives ahead, we'll dissect the art of distinguishing genuine love from its toxic imposter, focusing on the unique hurdles empathetic individuals face. Because honey, understanding is only half the battle; the real challenge lies in taking that knowledge and using it to pivot towards a healthier path. And it's about as easy as walking in stilettos on cobbled streets—but hey, who said we're not up for a challenge?

Embracing our worth goes beyond just walking away from what doesn't serve us; it's about embarking on a journey towards healing and self-love that's as enriching as a soul food Sunday dinner. We're talking about a transformation that leads to recognizing our inherent value, independent of any relationship status. It's about rebuilding that self-esteem brick by brick until it stands as sturdy as the Statue of Liberty.

So, let's get ready to lace up those emotional combat boots. We're about to march through the fog, beyond the battlefield of toxic love, moving steadfastly towards freedom. And believe me, by the end of this journey, we'll be sashaying into a life where we not only recognize toxic behaviors but summon the courage to say, "Thank you, next," with the confidence of a queen reigning supreme over her domain.

Honey, let's sit down and have a little heart-to-heart. You see, in this life, some things can get as complicated as trying to untangle headphones that have been mercilessly stuffed in the bottom of your bag. And one of those things, unfortunately, is love. Or more specifically, discerning love from manipulation. Now, don't get me wrong. Love is beautiful, powerful, and soul-filling. But when it starts to blend with manipulation, it turns into a fog so thick you can't see two steps ahead.

Consider this: love is supposed to lift you up, make you feel like you're soaring. But when manipulation creeps in, it's like suddenly those wings you felt spreading are being clipped, little by little, until you find yourself questioning whether you could ever fly at all. It's sneaky, like sugar in your grits when you were expecting salt – it just doesn't feel right. Manipulation twists words and actions into knots so elaborate you think you're losing your mind trying to figure out what's real and what isn't.

Now, imagine love and manipulation being ingredients in your mama's famous chili. Love is the beans – the hearty, nutritious base that keeps you coming back for more. Manipulation? That's the excessive salt. At first, you might not notice it, but too much of it, and the whole pot's ruined. You might keep eating, hoping that the next spoonful will be better, but deep down, you know something ain't right.

Understanding the blurred lines requires keen senses - the ability to taste the salt in the chili and say, "No more". It's noticing when sweet gestures come with strings attached or when apologies are just words tossed around to pacify, not to heal. Recognizing these signs isn't admitting defeat; it's reclaiming your power, your right to a love that lifts and supports, not one that binds and controls.

In essence, identifying the blurred lines between love and manipulation is like learning to trust your taste buds – knowing when something's too salty and having the courage to push the bowl away.

Now, why is it so damn hard for empathetic souls to spot these toxic behaviors? You know, being empathetic in a world that desperately needs it is like being that one umbrella in a downpour – everyone wants a piece, but too often, it leaves you catching all the rain. Empathetic individuals are like sponges; they absorb feelings, intentions, and emotions, focusing so much on healing others that they sometimes miss the signs of their own hurting.

It's like you're walking through that thick morning fog, armed with empathy as your guiding light. The problem? That same light tends to attract those who have learned to manipulate it for their own benefit, dimming it in the process. You see, empathetic people often give countless second chances, believing deeply in the good in others, sometimes to their own detriment. It's a tough spot, trying to differentiate between genuine mistakes and manipulation disguised as penitence.

Imagine empathy as a flashlight in the dark, revealing paths and dangers alike. Sometimes, to protect its glow, you've got to shield it, be selective about where it shines. Understanding this doesn't mean dimming your light or hardening your heart; it's about recognizing that not everyone deserves your warmth. It's learning to see the contrasts in the dark, to distinguish between who's there to help you hold the light and who's there to snuff it out.

Empathy in the hands of someone manipulative becomes a tool against you. It's like planning a garden party, only for someone to take advantage of your hard work to throw their own party, leaving you out of your own guest list. Recognizing this isn't giving up on empathy; it's refining it, ensuring it amplifies your life instead of dimming it.

Could understanding our own empathy be the key to unlocking our chains, giving us the clarity to see beyond the fog?

Now, let's talk courage - not the kind you see in movies, but real, raw courage. The kind it takes to prioritize your well-being over a toxic relationship. It's like deciding to leave a party early because you know it's not where you need to be. You might miss out on some fun, sure, but what you're really doing is choosing peace, choosing yourself.

Gathering that courage is like preparing for a harsh Jersey

winter. You know the storm's coming, so you start layering up, stocking up, and battening down the hatches. It's not about fearing the storm; it's about respecting your ability to weather it. Prioritizing your personal well-being means recognizing when the environment no longer serves you, no matter how familiar or comforting it seems.

It's as if you've been trying to grow roses in salted earth. No matter how much you care or what you do, they just won't bloom. Cultivating courage is the moment you decide to move your garden - it's acknowledging that you deserve fertile soil, a place where you can thrive free from toxicity.

Choosing yourself doesn't mean you never loved the other person. It means understanding that true love shouldn't cost you your peace, your joy, or your essence. It's about knowing that sometimes, the most loving thing you can do for yourself and the other person is to walk away, to allow each of you the space to grow in healthier environments.

Identifying the manipulation hidden within love, understanding the empathy that blinds us to it, and cultivating the courage to choose ourselves are the steps to breaking free from the fog of a toxic relationship.

Recognizing toxic behaviors in a relationship ain't no

easy feat, sis. It's like trying to find your keys in the dark—it's confusing, frustrating, and you might stub your toe a few times. But here's the tea: **for us empathetic queens, it's even trickier**. We see the good in folks like a heat-seeking missile, but sometimes that good is just a mirage in the desert of toxic love. **Don't beat yourself up if you've been tangled in this web, love, it happens to the best of us**.

Now, understanding the challenges we face is half the battle won. It's like knowing your opponent's playbook before a game—you're already steps ahead, babe. And cultivating that courage to say, "Bye, toxic boo, I'm choosing me," is a power move, a flex on those who thought they could dim your light. **You're a strong, fierce woman, and nobody can hold you back once you spread those wings**.

So, as we round up this chapter and slide into the next one, remember this: **recognizing toxicity ain't about pointing fingers, it's about self-love**. It's about reclaiming your energy and owning your worth. This journey ain't easy, but oh honey, the rewards are sweeter than Aunt May's peach cobbler on a summer day. So, buckle up, boo, 'cause we're just getting started on this ride to freedom and self-discovery.

Chapter 2: Reclaiming Self-Worth from the Shadows

As the sunlight crept through the blinds, casting zebra stripes across the linoleum floor, Jasmine sat at her kitchen table, nursing a mug of too-strong coffee. The morning's quiet was a stark contrast to the tempest in her mind. She traced her finger around the rim of the cup, her thoughts thick with the memories of last night's argument, the way every word from Darren felt like a chess move, strategic and designed to bring her king — her sense of self — into check.

She chuckled sourly, thinking about how she used to believe that love was supposed to lift you up, not yank the rug from beneath your feet. 'But there you go, girl, trippin' over love's tripwire,' she mused, recalling the times Darren had twisted her words, made her doubt her own heart, her memories. The smell of the eggs she had started to scramble filled the kitchen, but she wasn't hungry, her appetite another casualty of the confusion.

Down the street, kids laughed on their way to school, the

sound like a balm, a sweet reminder that innocence and joy still danced on the sidewalks outside her door. The laughter tiptoed into her chest, a slight itch of hope, connecting her to a "before" — when her laughter wasn't so scarce, her smiles not so hard-fought.

'When did his validation become the air you breathe, Jasmine?' she asked herself, annoyed and aware that she had let Darren's words become the gospel she lived by, the yardstick by which she measured her worth. Sifting through the relics of her past independence felt like trying to catch smoke — elusive and frustrating. The echo of her mother's voice came to her then, firm and wrapped in love, 'Baby, never give someone else the pen to write your story.'

She had to admit, though, that while her mother's words were the North Star, it took more than compasses to navigate the treacherous waters that she was in. She needed a ship sturdier than the one she was on, sails made from the fabric of her forgotten confidence. So, she stood, letting the morning be a signal for change. She pressed her hands flat on the table, grounding herself before opening the drawer that held the flyers for women's support groups she had collected and not called. The world outside beckoned, with all its thorny and beautiful possibilities. Her hands shook; it wasn't the caffeine.

As she fingered the edge of the flyer, toying with the idea of walking into a meeting, stating her name, and owning her story for the first time in what felt like forever, she let out a breath she didn't realize she was holding. A resolve settled over her like a shawl, and she decided she'd walk in those meetings wearing her best armor: her vulnerability.

She'd walk that path to rediscovering Jasmine, the one whose laughter was a hymn, and whose stride told stories of unwavering strength. Sure, it'd be a fight to claim herself from the shadows, but wasn't she her mama's daughter? The spirit in her voice, the firmness of her resolve, wasn't that proof enough that the phoenix inside her was just catching its breath before rising?

So, as Jasmine slips on her worn leather jacket, confronting the new day and its old troubles, consider this: when was the last time you picked up the pen and wrote a chapter of your life in your own hand?

Stepping Out of the Shadows

Honey, let me tell you, recognizing the cunning tactics of a toxic partner is like deciphering code—complicated but not impossible. These partners, bless their hearts, can be slicker than a wet driveway, using everything from gaslighting to emotional abuse to make you question your worth. It's a sneaky play, making you feel like you're the problem, twisting reality until you're unsure what's up or down. But here's the kicker: realizing this is your first step toward reclaiming your crown.

Understanding these tactics is essential. Toxic partners are experts at making you feel smaller than a pea in a pod, often so subtly that you don't notice until you're feeling down in the dumps. Recognizing this isn't about assigning blame but acknowledging what's been holding you back. It's like shining a bright light in a dark room and seeing the mess for what it is—a mess that isn't yours to clean up alone.

The journey to rebuild your self-worth starts with a solid yet simple foundation: **knowing your value is non-negotiable.** Envision your worth like a precious family heirloom; it doesn't decrease based on someone's inability to see its value. Rebuilding self-esteem is mending the cracks that toxic relationships have left, ensuring that your light shines bright, honey, unapologetically.

Learning to question and rebuild your identity outside of these draining dynamics is akin to taking a deep, soul-cleansing breath after being submerged underwater. It's exhilarating, scary, and liberating all at once. Remember, you were somebody before that relationship, and you'll continue to be somebody after. Rediscovering hobbies, passions, and dreams that were pushed aside is not just an act of self-care—it's a revolutionary act of self-love.

Developing strategies to counteract those pesky feelings of unworthiness is where the rubber meets the road. It's about switching up the narrative, telling yourself, "I am worthy, I am enough, and I got this," even when—especially when—that little voice of doubt wants to chime in. Surrounding yourself with a strong support system, seeking professional help, and practicing self-compassion are not just steps, they're leaps toward reasserting your mighty worth.

Remember, breaking free from toxic bonds isn't just about leaving a person; it's about escaping from the mindset and patterns that held you captive. It's stepping out of the shadows, blinking in the bright sunlight, and realizing you've been your superhero all along. Embrace the journey of self-discovery with all its twists and turns, knowing each step forward is a step toward the freedom you deserve.

And so, as you flip the pages of this journey, marinate on this: reclaiming your self-worth isn't just about healing from the past; it's about building a future where you are the master of your destiny, fierce and unbreakable. So, go on, put your crown back on, adjust it, and let the world see you sparkle.

Recognize the Tactics Used by Toxic Partners to Erode Self-Esteem

Honey, let's talk straight. Ever noticed how a toxic partner can make you question your own sanity? Like, one minute everything's sweet, and the next, you're spinning, trying to figure out up from down. That's their game – gaslighting. It's like they flip the script so smoothly, you start doubting your own memories and feelings. Crazy, right?

Imagine you're holding a big, beautiful mirror that reflects all the good stuff about you. Now, think of every put-down, every snide comment, every "you're too sensitive" as a crack in that mirror. Over time, those cracks multiply until it's hard to see your true reflection. That's what emotional abuse does. It chips away at your self-esteem, bit by bit, until you're left questioning your worth.

But, darling, it's all smoke and mirrors. These tactics – the gaslighting, the backhanded compliments, the constant criticism – they're tools in the abuser's kit. And why do they use them? To throw you off your game. To make you feel small. To keep you dependent on them for validation. It's like being trapped in a never-ending cycle of proving yourself worthy of their love and attention.

Now, think about a game of chess. You've got your pieces lined up, ready to make strategic moves. In a toxic relationship, though, it feels like you're always a step behind, constantly reacting instead of acting. That's because the game is rigged. Your partner's moves aren't about mutual growth; they're about control and keeping you in a place where you're always doubting yourself.

The key point? Recognizing these tactics is the first step towards reclaiming your self-worth.

Learn to Question and Rebuild One's Self-Worth and Identity Outside of the Relationship

So, you've peeped the game, and now it's time to rewrite the rules. You gotta start by questioning the narrative you've been fed. Who told you that you weren't enough? Spoiler alert: it wasn't you. It's like you've been wearing someone else's glasses, and surprise, surprise, the prescription ain't yours. It's blurry, distorted, and honestly, giving you a headache.

Rebuilding your self-worth starts with peeling off those labels that were never yours to wear. Think of it as decluttering your closet. You find pieces that don't fit, don't reflect who you are, or were given to you by someone who didn't really know your style. Toss 'em out, honey. Make room for the authentic you – the one who knows her worth doesn't come from someone else's approval.

Now, I want you to picture yourself as a beautiful, complex puzzle. Over time, toxic relationships can scatter your pieces, making you feel incomplete. The beauty, though, is in the rebuilding. Piece by piece, you start to see the whole picture. And guess what? You get to decide which pieces belong and which don't. It's empowering, realizing you are the master of your own puzzle.

Let me hit you with a little wisdom: questioning your self-worth and identity outside of a relationship is not a one-and-done deal. It's a journey, honey. Some days, you'll feel like you're moving mountains. Other days, it feels more like sifting through sand. But every step, every question, every moment of self-reflection, is moving you closer to yourself.

Letting go of someone else's idea of you is scary, sure, but it's also liberating. It's like stepping out of a room that's too small, into a world that's big enough to hold all your dreams, aspirations, and the full, fabulous scope of who you are.**So, what if the person you were meant to become is just on**

Develop Strategies to Counteract Feelings of Unworthiness and Reassert One's Value

Now, we're onto the good stuff. Developing strategies to kick those feelings of unworthiness to the curb? Yes, please. Think of this as putting together your comeback playlist – the one that has all the tracks that make you feel like you can conquer the world.

First things first, let's talk about affirmation. I don't mean the fluffy "you're a star!" kind (even though you are), but the deep, soul-touching affirmations that resonate with who you are at your core. It's like having a hype woman in your head, always ready to remind you of your magic, especially on those days when you're not feeling it.

Visualization is another powerhouse strategy. Picture yourself living that life you dream of – the one where you're not just surviving but thriving. This isn't about creating a fantasy world; it's about setting a vision for where you want to be. It's powerful, baby, because what the mind can see, it can achieve.

Now, let's talk boundaries. Honey, if you haven't set them yet, now's the time. Boundaries aren't about pushing people away; they're about protecting your energy. It's like building a fence around your fabulous garden, not to block the view but to ensure that only those who respect the space get to enjoy it.

Lastly, community. Surround yourself with folks who lift you up, who see you for who you are and not just who you can be to them. This tribe, this chosen family, is crucial. They're the net that catches you when you fall and the push that propels you further than you thought possible.

Together, these strategies are your arsenal in the ongoing journey of reclaiming your self-worth and audaciously asserting your value in every space you occupy.

Alright, sis, we've dived deep into the murky waters of toxic relationships. We've peeled back the layers to expose the tactics used to chip away at our confidence and self-worth. But guess what? We ain't staying in those shadows!

Recognize how those toxic partners try to dim your light, how they use gaslighting and emotional abuse to make you question your worth. Don't let their negativity rent space in your mind, evict that mess!

Learn to love yourself fiercely outside of their toxicity.

Rediscover the beauty, strength, and magic that's uniquely you. You're a whole vibe all on your own, darling, and no one can take that from you.

Develop your arsenal of strategies to fight back against feeling unworthy. Surround yourself with love, affirmations, and people who uplift you. You are a Queen, crown shining bright, and anyone who can't see that can step to the left, honey!

So, as we close this chapter, remember this: You are worthy beyond measure. Your value doesn't diminish because someone else failed to see it. Stand tall in your worth, walk away from toxicity with your head held high, and embrace the freedom that comes with reclaiming your self-worth. The journey to healing and self-love isn't always easy, but oh, is it worth it!

Chapter 3: The Courage to Walk Away: Embracing Self-Preservation

In the muted light of her kitchen, Ava stood by the window, watching droplets freckle the glass in an unruly rhythm—a rain that offered a cleanse from the outside looking in. Water wept down the panes, and within those trails, she saw the possibility of washing away old wounds. Time seemed to move in sync with the trickle of rain; fast, persistent, unstoppable. It was a Tuesday afternoon that felt no different from the one before, yet to Ava, it carried the weight of a lifetime.

As she sipped her coffee, strong and black like the women who raised her, Ava whispered to herself, "Girl, your love should not be a battlefield." The mug warmed her hands, even as her chest harbored a cold knot of realization. She had decided. Today was the day she would gather the remnants of her heart and choose herself over the chaos that waited dormant in the other room, veiled by temporary tranquility.

He was still asleep, peaceful in a way that never reached her anymore. Remembering the way he'd effortlessly charm her and then unravel that charm with sharp words left invisible scars on her spirit. Ava knew that love shouldn't hurt like this, shouldn't make her tiptoe in her own skin. "This ain't living," she muttered.

Her fingers toyed with the frayed edge of the kitchen towel, each unraveling thread mirroring pieces of her patience. Her resolve burst through her like the break of dawn, a radiant sun rising against the oppression of the night. Ava had cultivated resilience in the fertile ground of old pains and disappointments. And, with a silent prayer, she steeled herself to sever the roots of a love entangling her breath, her being.

Neighborhood sounds wafted through the barely cracked window, muffled conversations and laughter from the street below, life moving, blood flowing. It reminded her that there was a world out there, full of fresh air and new mornings. A world that didn't confine her to the shrinking walls of a love poisoned by control, a world where her worth was defined by her own damn self, and not by the hands that now slept in the next room.

The weight of her decision anchored her, yet she floated on the edge of a dream. Could standing up for her peace be the bridge to a life where she was the artist of her canvas, not the subject of another's distorted portrait? Could the heavy door she was about to walk through lead to a garden where self-love was the only seed sown? Her heart broke and bloomed in that slender moment. She was about to find out if the courage that pulsed in her veins could outshine the fear that clung like ivy to her mind.

"Is walking away the hardest dance, or the first step to the music of my soul?" she wondered, as the aroma of rain and brewing coffee lingered like the echo of soon-to-be-forgotten footsteps.

Honey, Let's Talk About Walking Away

Walking away from a toxic relationship isn't about admitting defeat—it's about claiming victory over your own life. This chapter is sincerely dedicated to every soul out there feeling trapped in a cycle that dims their shine, making you forget the vibrant, valued being you were meant to be. The United States, might be our physical locale, but this journey transcends geographical boundaries—it's about traversing the landscapes of our hearts and minds.

Let's keep it real for a moment. Society loves to paint leaving as an act of cowardice. They'll have you thinking that sticking it out, no matter how damaging, is a badge of honor. But often, what's left unsaid speaks volumes. Take the story of grandma and grandpa, for instance. Everyone loves to romanticize their over 50 years together, glorifying their resilience through thick and thin. Yet, they conveniently omit the painful truths. They don't talk about how grandpa was a rolling stone, leaving heartaches in his wake with four children born outside their marriage. Nor do they mention how he was rarely home, his presence more a whisper than a stronghold in their lives. Sure, he paid the bills, but at what cost to grandma's heart, her dreams? Let me tell you, there's nothing heroic about sacrificing your well-being, your dreams, or your happiness for the sake of appearances. It's high time we redefine what it means to walk away. It's not giving up; it's **standing up**—for yourself, your health, your happiness, and your future.

Challenge those societal stigmas, girl. They're outdated narratives that don't serve anyone, least of all you. When you decide to leave a toxic relationship, you're not broadcasting failure; you're announcing to the world—and more importantly, to yourself—that you know your worth. You recognize that no one should settle for a half-lived life, marred by emotional turmoil.

Reframing leaving as an act of self-love and empowerment is where the magic happens. It's about shifting that perspective from loss to gain—from losing a partner to gaining back your sense of self. Let's call it what it is: a bold, revolutionary act of self-care. It's choosing to prioritize your happiness, peace, and health over remaining entangled in a web that saps your strength and dims your light.

Building resilience to overcome the fear and guilt of ending a toxic relationship is crucial. We all know it's easier said than done, especially when you're bombarded with 'should haves' and 'what ifs.' But here's the thing—you've got a well of strength inside of you. It's about tapping into that strength, step by tentative step, until you're standing on solid ground, fear and guilt underfoot.

So, how do you build that resilience? Start with small acts of self-care and self-love. Surround yourself with a support system that sees your worth—even when you're struggling to see it yourself. Celebrate each small victory, each day that you choose yourself. And remember, it's okay to seek professional help to guide you through this journey. Let's debunk a myth that's been holding us back for too long: the outdated notion that seeking therapy brands you as 'crazy' for life. This is far from the truth. In reality, choosing to see a therapist is a sign of strength and self-awareness. It's about taking control of your journey and being brave enough to seek understanding and healing. Far from a life-long label, it's a step towards a life filled with greater self-awareness, healing, and emotional freedom. Healing is not a linear process; it's a series of ups and downs, but every step forward is a step toward reclaiming your life.

At the heart of this chapter is a simple, yet powerful message: you are worthy. Worthy of love that uplifts, not tears down. Worthy of a life filled with joy, not sorrow. Worthy of relationships that are rooted in mutual respect, understanding, and genuine affection. So, if you're on the fence, let this be your sign. It's time to unapologetically choose yourself. Because, my dear, walking away isn't the end—it's the beginning of a beautiful, new chapter.

We all know the feeling, right? You're at a family reunion in Carolina, and Auntie leans over, giving you that look, asking, "When are you going to settle down?" or "Why did you let that good man go?" It's like there's this unspoken rule that if you're not tethered to someone, then something's wrong with you. Society's got this playbook that dictates staying in a relationship, no matter how rocky, is a testament to your character. But let's cut through that noise right here. Walking away from a situation that dims your light isn't defeat; it's declaring your worth.

Imagine you're wearing a pair of shoes that's way too tight. Sure, they look stunning on the outside, but every step is a painful reminder that they just don't fit. You try to ignore the discomfort, telling yourself that beauty is pain, right? Wrong. This is what sticking around in a toxic relationship feels like. On the outside, things might seem fine, but it's squeezing the life out of you. Shedding those painful 'shoes' is the first step toward walking a path that's right for you—a journey toward healing and self-discovery.

Now, I know what some might say, "But breaking up means giving up," or, "You didn't try hard enough." But let's set the records straight. It takes guts to recognize that you're in a harmful situation and even more courage to step away from it. According to a report by the American Psychological Association, individuals who leave toxic relationships report a significant increase in well-being and a decrease in stress levels. That screams empowerment to me, not failure.

Yet, here we stand, caught between the devil and the deep blue sea, swayed by whispers of tradition and the daunting waves of societal expectation. The truth, however, is as clear as day: choosing to leave a toxic relationship is akin to choosing yourself. It's about putting your happiness and mental health at the forefront, where it belongs.

Choosing self-love by leaving a toxic relationship isn't giving up; it's a powerful statement that you value your peace and happiness above societal expectations.

Let's flip the script. Instead of viewing the end of a relationship as the curtain call on your love life, consider it the grand opening of a new chapter—your chapter. Leaving doesn't just mean walking out the door; it's a declaration of independence, a celebration of self-love, and honestly, the most badass move you could make.

Ever watch a movie where the protagonist finally stands up to the antagonist? It's that moment of truth, the climax, where they choose themselves over the turmoil. That's you. You're the hero of your story. Making the bold decision to leave a toxic relationship is like that final cinematic showdown—except the victory is a more peaceful heart and a freer soul.

But how do you reframe leaving as an act of self-love? It begins with understanding that self-love isn't selfish; it's necessary. Think of it this way: if you're running on empty, how can you possibly give to others? You can't pour from an empty cup. Prioritizing your well-being sets a foundation for healthier relationships in the future, with others and, most importantly, with yourself.

The self-empowerment doesn't stop with the decision to

leave. It continues as you rebuild your sense of self, outside of a relationship that once defined you. Each step you take towards healing and rediscovering your joy and passions is a testament to your resilience. It's not about finding someone new to complete you but about reassembling the pieces of yourself into the masterpiece you've always been.

Remember, empowerment is recognizing when a situation no longer serves you and having the courage to say "enough." It's about setting boundaries and respecting yourself enough to enforce them. This journey of self-love isn't an easy one, but nothing worth having ever is. Building a life on your own terms, filled with love and respect that begins within, isn't just liberating; it's transformative.

Could recognizing your worth and asserting it by leaving a toxic relationship be the most groundbreaking love story you'll ever write?

Now, let's talk about building resilience. I know, the thought of leaving can summon a tag team of fear and guilt, pounding at the door of your heart with each deliberation. But here's the thing about resilience—it's not about not feeling the fear and guilt; it's about facing them head-on and deciding your peace is worth the fight.

Foresee resilience as a muscle. Just like in the gym, the more you work it, the stronger it becomes. Every time you reaffirm your decision to choose peace over turmoil, you're doing a resilience rep. You're building that inner strength, that fortitude to weather the storm and emerge on the other side, not just intact but invigorated.

It's a lot like preparing for a hurricane. You know it's coming; the air is tense, heavy with the weight of impending tumult. But instead of letting the fear consume you, you secure your windows, stock up on supplies, and create a safety plan. This preparation doesn't negate the hurricane's impact, but it does fortify you against it. Similarly, anticipating the challenges of leaving and strategizing your path to healing is an exercise in resilience. It won't make the process painless, but it will make you powerful in your pursuit of peace.

One step at a time, you start to realize that the fear and guilt, though daunting, don't hold a candle to the promise of a future where you are the master of your destiny. You begin to understand that this process is not just about survival but about thriving, redefining your identity on your own terms, and reclaiming your narrative.**Challenging societal stigmas, reframing leaving as an act of self-love, and building resilience are not just steps toward leaving a toxic relationship. They are leaps toward embracing your worth, prioritizing your peace, and, ultimately,**

crafting a life filled with self-respect and happiness. You don't just walk away from something; you're walking towards the person you were always meant to be.

Leaving a toxic relationship ain't about giving up, sis. It's about taking charge of your life like the boss queen you are. **Challenging the haters who say otherwise**, and flipping the script to see walking away as an act of self-love and empowerment is where it's at. **You're not failing; you're thriving** by choosing your well-being over toxic ties.

Refocus your lens, sis. Leaving ain't a weakness; it's reclaiming your power. Society might throw shade, but you're shining bright in your self-preservation glow. It's not about what they think; it's about owning your truth and valuing yourself enough to say, "I deserve better."

Now, building up that armor against fear and guilt is key. **Drown out the doubters** with self-assurance and resilience. **Let that courage you're fueling** push you past those doubts and out into the light of your own self-worth. Stand tall, knowing that choosing YOU is never the wrong move.

So, when it's time to step away from toxicity, remember this: **You're breaking free to stand stronger**, to love deeper, and to live authentically. Your path to freedom starts with valuing yourself enough to say, "I'm worth more than this."

And trust me, hun, you are.

Chapter 4: Boundary Building and the Art of Self-Care

Outside, an autumn wind tousled the fallen leaves along the streets of Ewing. That same wind whispered through the cracks of an old cafe window where Jordan sat, a steaming cup of coffee warming her hands. Her eyes followed the trails of steam as she contemplated her next step. She had been here before, in the dappled sunlight of the cafe, where the scent of roasted beans was a balm to rattled nerves. But today, her thoughts were heavy, entwined with the memories of a love that once felt like salvation but had turned into a cage.

The bell over the cafe door jingled, pulling Jordan from her reverie. With a glance, she acknowledged the newcomer, but her mind was still miles away, wrestling with boundaries—those she should have erected long ago and those she was now determined to build. She took a slow sip, letting the warm liquid fortify her resolve. Boundaries, she thought, they're not walls to keep joy out, but shields to keep a bruised heart safe.

An old friend had once told her, "You cannot pour from an empty cup," and it rang true as a church bell on Sunday morning. Self-care seemed like a foreign concept, something luxurious and out of reach, but Jordan had come to understand it was her right, her necessity. She had loved, and in doing so, she had lost herself piece by piece, fitting into the mold of another's needs. But no more.

She began to sketch plans in her notebook—her personalized self-care plan. It wasn't about spa days or splurging on fancy things, though those were nice. No, this was about respect—self-respect. It was about saying 'no' when she was worn, about honoring her emotions and making space for her healing.

"Excuse me, may I borrow the sugar?" The man at the adjacent table smiled kindly. Jordan passed the sugar with a steady hand, reclaiming her space when he lingered a bit too long. Setting boundaries was a practice, a daily, sometimes minute-by-minute, commitment.

As she sat there, the setting sun casting long shadows across the floor of the cafe, a peace settled in her chest. It was the understanding that caring for herself wasn't a retreat from life; it was an embrace of it, with all its trials and its triumphs. And as the city wrapped its arms around the night, Jordan knew she was beginning the tender work of coming home to herself.

But as she slipped her coat on and faced the brisk evening air, she had to wonder: when the time comes to defend those newly established boundaries, will she stand firm, or will the familiar patterns of the past beckon her back into their fold?

As Jordan stepped out into the brisk evening air, her breath formed small clouds in the twilight. The world outside felt like a mirror of her internal landscape—crisp, clear, yet filled with the potential for change. With each step, she felt the weight of her past, a past where boundaries were as thin as paper and just as easily torn. But she was not that person anymore.

Walking down the lamp-lit streets of Ewing, Jordan reflected on the boundaries she had set. She knew that maintaining them wouldn't be easy. The old, familiar patterns of the past, like shadows, might try to creep back into her life. But this time, she felt armed with a new resolve, a strength born from self-awareness and the courage to prioritize her well-being.

She remembered the words of her therapist, spoken in a room filled with soft light and understanding, "Boundaries aren't just about saying no, they're about saying yes to what truly matters to you." Jordan had always been the one to bend, to accommodate, to erase parts of herself for the sake of others. But now, she understood that her needs mattered too.

As she passed the little bookstore where she used to browse with forgotten friends, a sense of empowerment grew within her. It was in these moments of solitude that she found clarity. Yes, there would be moments of doubt, times when the urge to revert to old patterns would be strong. But Jordan was learning that the act of setting boundaries was also an act of self-love. It wasn't just about guarding against others; it was about honoring her inner voice, her needs, and her values.

The cold wind brushed against her face, a reminder that change was constant. With each determined step, Jordan felt more in tune with herself. She had begun this journey thinking that setting boundaries would isolate her, but she was realizing it was doing the opposite. It was teaching her who her true allies were, those who respected her limits and cherished her for who she really was.

Let's Talk Boundaries, Shall We?

Imagine this scene: You're walking through the heart of your city, the gentle sunlight kissing your face, when it strikes you like a bolt of lightning. You've been giving every ounce of your energy to others, bending over backward to maintain harmony, that you've scarcely kept a drop for yourself. You feel like a car forever on the brink of empty, cruising miles without knowing your destination. Does this resonate with you? If so, darling, you're in good company. But let's be clear, it's high time we turn the page.

In a world where we're often told to put on a brave face and keep pushing forward, **establishing and enforcing personal boundaries** comes off as a revolutionary act. It's like owning your space in this crazy world and saying, "This is where I end, and you begin, and that's okay." It sounds simple, right? But for anyone who's been in a toxic relationship, you know that boundaries might as well be a foreign concept. Your needs, desires, and preferences are often steamrolled in favor of keeping the peace or appeasing your partner. But here's where the plot twist comes in—reclaiming your agency and rebuilding your self-respect starts with laying down those boundary lines, brick by brick.

But hold up, let's not get ahead of ourselves. Before we can talk about drawing lines, we need to understand what boundaries even look like. We're talking about **Understanding Personal Boundaries** here. It's about taking a hard look at what you value, what you need, and what you won't stand for, then communicating that with the confidence of a queen. It's not about building walls; it's about opening doors—the ones that lead to respect, mutual understanding, and genuine connection.

Next, we waltz into the soothing rhythm of **Self-Care Practices for Healing**. Now, I know when people mention self-care, you might be thinking of bubble baths and face masks—and hey, if that's your jam, more power to you. But self-care is also about diving deep into what lights your soul on fire. It's about giving yourself the love, respect, and attention that you've been pouring out so freely to others. It's mindfulness, journaling, hitting the gym, or even just sitting quietly with a good book. And let's not forget about that support network. Having folks who get it, who uplift you, and remind you of your worth in those moments of doubt? Priceless.

But we're not stopping there. We're moving on up to **Building Self-Respect and Recovery**. This is where the real work happens. It's about setting goals, no matter how small, and celebrating every single victory. It's about challenging that inner critic, the one that whispers you're not good enough, and saying, "Not today." It's about growth, learning, and pushing beyond those old stories we've told ourselves about who we are and what we deserve.

The Blueprint to Boundaries and Beyond

Step 1: Understanding Personal Boundaries

- Reflect on your values and needs. This isn't just about knowing what you like; it's about recognizing what makes you feel respected and valued.
- Identify past boundary breaches. Think about when you felt disrespected or undervalued. Use those feelings as your compass.
- Communicate assertively. It's more than just speaking up; it's about being heard. Express your needs with conviction.
- Enforce those boundaries. When they're crossed, have a game plan. It might mean having to cut back on time with certain folks, and that's okay.

Step 2: Self-Care Practices for Healing

- Dabble in different self-care activities. Find what soothes your soul and lights you up.
- Create a self-care schedule. Make it as routine as your morning coffee.

- Be kind to yourself. On those hard days, remember you're doing just fine.
- Surround yourself with your squad. Those folks who lift you higher? Keep them close.

Step 3: Building Self-Respect and Recovery

- Celebrate your wins. Big or small, a win is a win.
- Challenge negative self-talk. Replace "I can't" with "Watch me."
- Seek growth. Whether it's classes or new hobbies, find what excites you.
- Forgive and let go. Holding onto past hurt? Release it. You've got too much brightness ahead to be looking back.

So there you have it, darling. It's about carving out that space for yourself, respecting it, and filling it with all the love, care, and joy you've been handing out to everyone else. It's time to take that stroll down the streets of the city, head held high, knowing exactly where you end and others begin. And maybe, just maybe, you'll find that the journey to freedom starts with the courage to say, "This is me, and I'm worth it."

Learn to Establish and Enforce Personal Boundaries

In the hustle and bustle of the city, just like in your personal life, everyone's got a space they call their own. You wouldn't let someone walk into your home and start rearranging your furniture, would you? That's because your home is your personal space, your boundary. Similarly, in relationships, setting boundaries is like drawing a circle around your emotional, physical, and psychological space and saying, "This is mine." It's a fundamental step in not just healing from emotional abuse but in building any healthy relationship.

But honey, establishing boundaries? Now that's a process. It's like learning to dance; at first, you might step on a few toes or feel a bit awkward, but with practice, you'll be setting boundaries like a pro, moving through life with grace. It begins with understanding what you value, what your needs are, and what you can and cannot tolerate. This clarity is your compass, guiding you in drawing those lines clearly and confidently.

Enforcing these boundaries, though, that's where the rubber meets the road. It's not enough to just state what your boundaries are; you need to stick to them, even when it's tough, even when it feels like you're the only one standing in your corner. Picture it like a garden fence. Sure, it might seem a little off-putting at first, but it's what keeps the things you cherish safe and allows what's inside to flourish. When someone attempts to overstep those boundaries, it's like someone trying to climb over your garden fence. You have the right, no, the responsibility, to stand up and reinforce that fence, ensuring your well-being remains protected.

Now, I'm not saying this is easy, not by a long shot. There will be times when you'll want to bend those boundaries for the sake of peace or out of fear of losing someone. But remember, anyone who truly respects and values you will understand and honor the boundaries you set. And those who don't? Well, baby, they're showing you that they don't deserve a space in your garden in the first place.

In the end, the key point to remember is that setting and enforcing boundaries is about respecting and valuing yourself enough to guard your well-being, just as you would protect your home in.

Understanding Personal Boundaries

First things first, take a minute and think about what matters most to you, what sets your soul on fire, and where your peace of mind begins and ends. This is about getting real with yourself about what you value, your needs, and especially your limits. Just like when you're picking out what to wear for a night out—you know what fits, what's comfortable, and what's a straight-up no. Use that awareness to spell out your boundaries for others.

Reflecting on past experiences where your boundaries might have been trespassed can be a game changer. Remember that time when someone crossed the line, and how it left you feeling? Yeah, that discomfort, anger, or sadness is your heart's way of saying, "No more!" Use these feelings as signposts for setting firmer boundaries moving forward.

Now, talking about boundaries can feel as intimidating as stepping up to the mic at that jazz spot on 5th, but it's got to be done. Communicate your boundaries with the same confidence and assertiveness as if you were asking for your favorite drink at the bar—straight, no chaser. This is about being clear, direct, and unwavering in expressing your needs and limits.

But what happens when someone tries to push past those limits, treating your boundaries like suggestions rather than non-negotiables? Honey, that's when you need to be ready to enforce those boundaries, laying out the consequences with the same determination and finesse as a diva commanding the stage. Whether it means taking a step back from someone or ending a conversation, be prepared to do what's necessary to protect your peace.

Self-Care Practices for Healing

Self-care is not a luxury; it's a necessity, especially when you're walking the path of healing from emotional scars. Think of it like applying the richest, most nurturing lotion to dry skin; it's about nourishing yourself from the inside out. Whether it's hitting the gym with your squad, finding your Zen in meditation, writing down your thoughts and dreams, or simply doing more of what makes your heart sing, self-care is your power move.

Now listen up, creating a self-care plan isn't about sprinkling a few random acts of kindness toward yourself here and there. It's about building a routine, a ritual that puts you at the top of your to-do list every single day. Picture it as crafting the ultimate playlist—one that's got the right mix of tunes to lift you up and keep you moving, no matter what. Schedule these self-care activities into your day like VIP events, because, babe, you are the VIP.

In this journey, be your own hype woman. Talk to yourself with love, kindness, and compassion, reminding yourself that healing is a marathon, not a sprint. Surround yourself with people who lift you up, who get your story because they've got chapters of their own. This squad is your backup singers, there to support you every step of the way.

Ask yourself, what does it mean for you to truly care for yourself after surviving emotional turmoil?

Creating a Personalized Self-Care Plan That Champions Self-Respect and Recovery

Envision self-care as the art of creating the ideal cup of coffee on a brisk morning—it's about selecting the perfect blend that provides warmth and prepares you for the day ahead. Within this framework, we're aiming to brew the ultimate cup, one that delights the taste buds and simultaneously nourishes you, both heart and soul.

Understanding Boundaries

Just like understanding the various coffee beans and their flavors is key to a great brew, recognizing the importance of boundaries is foundational. This step involves identifying those areas in your life where boundaries can create a safe and nurturing space, just as the right coffee bean selection sets the tone for your morning.

Identifying Personal Boundaries

Now, think about what suits your palate. Is it the bold richness of a dark roast or the light, floral notes of a blonde roast? Similarly, reflecting on your own values, needs, and comfort zones allows you to outline what your personal boundaries look like. This self-reflection is akin to choosing your preferred coffee beans for the perfect cup that suits you uniquely.

Communicating Boundaries

Once you've got a handle on your preferred blend, you wouldn't hesitate to tell your barista, right? Likewise, this step is about articulating your boundaries clearly and assertively to those around you. It's about expressing your needs and expectations in a way that's understood, respected, and valued.

Enforcing Boundaries

Your morning coffee ritual is sacred; you wouldn't let anyone mess with it. So, when it comes to boundaries, staying firm and consistent is key. Enforcing your boundaries might involve making tough decisions or standing your ground, much like insisting on the quality of your morning brew, regardless of others' preferences.

The Power of Self-Care

Imagine your personalized self-care plan as the cream and sugar to your coffee. It's what makes the experience not just bearable but delightful. This step focuses on incorporating those activities that nurture and replenish your physical, mental, and spiritual being. It's about enriching your cup of life with practices that make every sip count.

Creating a Personalized Self-Care Plan

And finally, creating your personalized self-care plan is about blending all these elements together into a routine that suits your life's rhythm perfectly. It means regularly engaging in those activities that fill your cup, ensuring you're not just going through the motions but truly enjoying every moment of your day.

By embracing both boundary setting and self-care, you're not just surviving; you're thriving, turning your past pain into the grounds for a rich, fulfilling future.

Setting boundaries and prioritizing self-care ain't just a suggestion; it's a recipe for takin' back your power and finding your worth. Your boundaries are like the velvet ropes at the club—you decide who gets in and who's left waiting outside. You deserve respect, love, and care, and ain't no one gonna make you feel otherwise. **Self-care ain't just bubble baths and face masks; it's a revolutionary act of reclaiming your joy and peace.** Remember, you can't pour from an empty cup, so fill yours up with all the good stuff that makes you thrive. **Craftin' your personal self-care plan ain't just a task; it's a love letter to yourself, a promise to cherish and uplift your spirit.** Don't shy away from doin' what sets your soul on fire and nourishes your heart; you deserve every bit of that goodness. By building strong boundaries and making self-care a non-negotiable, you're sculpting a sanctuary within yourself where peace, love, and freedom reign supreme. Your journey to healin' begins with you showin' up for yourself every single day, no compromises.

Chapter 5: Finding Strength in Unity: Leveraging Support Systems

She stirred her tea, the clink of the spoon against the ceramic mug echoed in the silence of her kitchen. Sunlight spilled onto the worn countertop, casting a warm glow on the array of plants basking in its touch. It was a typical Thursday morning, yet nothing seemed typical for Ebony. Amidst the peaceful setting, her mind was a battleground, replaying the hurtful words and the cold indifference she had grown too familiar with.

She remembered the laughter, the shared dreams that now seemed like a distant whisper, lost to the night. But alongside the sweet, the bitter had taken root, and the once beautiful garden of their love was now overgrown with the thorny brambles of neglect and manipulation. It was supposed to be a partnership, a dance of two souls in step, not this twisted parody where her voice was drowned beneath the cacophony of his ego.

Her aunt Tasha had always said, "Honey, a man's words ain't no heavier than the truth they're anchored to," and Ebony knew the truth hadn't been present for a long time. Friends would telephone, their voices a lifeline, pulling her towards shores of comfort and solidarity. They offered ears that would listen without judgment and hearts generous with compassion. She couldn't help but smile, though. Leave it to her tribe to turn even the darkest moments into something that felt like a Sunday family dinner – nourishing and full of real talk.

As Ebony sipped her tea, feeling the warmth spread through her, she could hear her grandmother's sage voice, "Child, what's for you, won't pass by you." It was time to foster connections both in and outside her four walls that acknowledged her worth, the kind that sparked change, fanned flames of ambition, and sang songs of affirmation. Her Grandmama's hands, worn with time and love, always wrapped around hers when she needed strength to move past life's trials.

She needed to envelop herself in networks that knew her name and her story. Networks like the sister circle at the community center that pivoted from spoken word nights to healing circles. They were a reminder that she was not a solitary note but part of a symphony. A counsel that could show her the path she knew she had the right to walk – one where emotional bruises could heal and dignity, once stowed away, could soar once more.

And so, Ebony pondered, setting her empty mug down with a soft clink. If true strength was in the gathering of voices that sang with you, understood the tremor in your tone, and swayed with you through life's sordid verses, then wasn't it time she started harmonizing with those who played life's symphony in her key? Ain't it time to step out of the shadows and into the sunshine with folks who got her back?

Who's Got Your Back?

Now, let's get real for a moment. Navigating away from a toxic relationship is like detangling headphones that have been sitting in your drawer for too long. You know it's going to be a challenge, but honey, the reward is sweet silence or in this case, peace. In Piscataway aka Pway, my hometown, just like in any corner of this world, finding your tribe – that group of friends, family, or therapists who stands by you through thick and thin – is pivotal. It's all about **finding strength in unity**.

This chapter dives deep into the essence of support systems. I'm talking about the kind of support that gives you

emotional validation when you're questioning your every move, the **guidance** when you're lost, and that **sense of community** that reminds you you're not alone in this journey. Whether you find solace in sharing your story over coffee at Dunkin' on Washington Ave or find strength in the quiet moments with your therapist at a clinic on Stelton, it's all about making connections that heal.

First things first, identifying these supportive networks and resources is key. Not every friend or family member will understand, and that's okay. It's about quality, not quantity. Look for people who listen without judgment, offer empathy, and, most importantly, respect your journey. Sometimes, support comes from unexpected places. Support groups and therapy sessions can become sanctuaries of healing. Plain and simple, it's about finding your people, the ones who get it.

Now, let's chat about the magic of **emotional validation**. It's like the soul food of the healing process. When someone validates your feelings, it's an affirmation that what you're experiencing is real, and you're not 'overreacting'. In the heart of Piscataway, or anywhere really, finding spaces where your feelings are acknowledged is like finding gold. It's about reminding yourself that your emotions are valid, and you deserve to be heard.

Fostering connections that empower and encourage personal growth is where the real growth happens. It's about surrounding yourself with people who uplift you, inspire you, and push you to be your best self. Think of it like having your personal cheer squad in the stands at a high school football game, rooting for you, every step of the way. These connections are precious. They remind you of your worth, inspire you to set boundaries, and ultimately, they aid in reclaiming your life.

Navigating away from toxic relationships and healing from emotional abuse is not something you have to do alone. Your support system is your backbone. Whether it's a late-night heart-to-heart in your living room or an empowering session with your therapist, these connections form the foundation for your escape to freedom.

Remember, darlings, it's about understanding that you are worthy of love, respect, and all the good things life has to offer. Embracing your support system is embracing a journey towards healing, self-love, and rediscovery. So, let's raise a glass to finding strength in unity and marching towards freedom, one step at a time.

In the heart of the city, where the community weaves through every individual's story, the power of a supportive network cannot be overstated. It's like sitting on the porch with your closest family and friends, where the atmosphere is ripe with understanding, and the air vibrates with shared strength. Identifying these networks when you're tangled up in toxic relationships is akin to finding a beacon in the foggy night. Support systems, whether they stem from family, friends, or professional help, provide more than just an ear for your troubles; they offer validation, guidance, and a renewal of strength.

Imagine, if you will, a lighthouse standing steadfast on the shore. That's your support system. Amid turbulent seas and stormy relationships, it's what guides you home. Just knowing it's there - that your people are your lighthouse - can make all the difference when the night feels darkest. Now, finding these networks isn't always a walk in the park; sometimes, you've got to dig deep and actively seek them out. This could mean reconnecting with old friends, joining support groups, or maybe even finding solace in online communities where folks share your experiences and struggles.

Let's not forget the professional lifelines hanging out in plain sight: therapists, counselors, and life coaches. These are the folks equipped with the tools to not only listen but to help you navigate through your experiences. They hold space for you to unravel your feelings and thoughts without judgment, offering strategies and insights that can light up your path

ahead. Think of them as that friend who always has the tea –
the one who gives you the tough love you need to hear,
backed by wisdom to help you grow.

The truth is, support systems are everywhere once you start
looking. They could be sitting right next to you at the local
coffee shop, hidden in plain view. The key is opening up,
reaching out, and letting those connections into your life.
Well, that and knowing what you stand for, so you recognize
when others stand with you too.

**Finding the right support network is your beacon of
hope, guiding you through the stormy seas of toxic
relationships toward the haven of healing and strength.**

Connecting with supportive networks is one thing, but
understanding the role of emotional validation they provide is
like uncovering a hidden superpower. Imagine for a moment
that your feelings are seeds. When they're validated by
someone who genuinely supports you, it's as if those seeds
are watered, given sunlight, comforted by the soil. Over time,
they grow, they bloom, into a garden of self-worth and
resilience. Emotional validation acknowledges the legitimacy
of our experiences and emotions, affirming that what we feel
is real and significant.

Throwing around terms like "emotional validation" might sound like something straight out of a psychology textbook, but it's actually straight-up common sense when you break it down. It's about hearing, "I see you, I hear you, and what you're feeling makes sense." In the whirlwind that is escaping a toxic relationship, these words can be a lifeline, a confirmation that you're not overreacting or being overly sensitive. You're feeling just as you should. And that's okay.

This validation is pivotal in the healing process. It reinforces our sense of self and encourages emotional healing. It's akin to having a soul food dinner with your family. Just as every dish on the table nourishes you, each word of validation feeds your soul, helping you to mend bit by bit. Validation doesn't erase the pain, but it empowers you to face it, understand it, and eventually move beyond it.

However, it's crucial to differentiate supportive validation from empty platitudes. True validation doesn't skirt around the edges of your feelings; it dives deep, acknowledges the messy, the hard, and the uncomfortable. It comes from those genuine connections that you've identified and fostered, willing to get into the trenches with you. And let me tell you, when you find those people? Hold onto them tight.

Deep connections that offer genuine emotional validation create a sanctuary. They offer a shield against further emotional harm and nurture the resilience needed to break free from toxicity.

How might recognizing and seeking out emotional validation transform your journey toward healing?

Fostering connections that empower and encourage personal growth is like planting a garden in the fertile soil of Jersey. You wouldn't just throw seeds on the ground and hope for the best, right? No, you'd prepare the soil, you'd choose your seeds carefully, and you'd nurture them with water and sunlight. The same careful cultivation applies to building connections that support your growth.

These are the relationships that challenge you to be the best version of yourself. They cheer you on but aren't afraid to call you out when you need it. These are the people who throw a little shade just to remind you to keep it real, but also shine their light on you, basking you in warmth and understanding. Finding and nurturing this kind of connection requires intention and effort. It's about recognizing those who genuinely want the best for you and making the choice to grow together.

Let's get real for a second - not all connections serve this purpose. Some are like weeds in your garden, draining resources and suffocating your growth. Recognizing which relationships empower you and which ones hold you back is key. It's not about cutting people off left and right, but more about investing your energy into connections that uplift you.

Empowerment flows from connections that respect your boundaries, celebrate your achievements, and encourage your autonomy. It's the friend who insists you apply for that job because they know you'd slay it, or the family member who always has your back, reminding you of your worth when you forget.

By fostering these connections, you're essentially building a personal board of directors for your life—an ensemble cast of mentors, friends, and allies who guide you, inspire you, and help you navigate the ups and downs with grace and strength.

Identifying supportive networks, understanding the importance of emotional validation, and fostering empowering connections are cornerstones in building a foundation strong enough to not only escape toxic relationships but to thrive beyond them.

In A Nutshell: Finding your tribe, your crew, your ride-or-dies, can make all the difference in your journey to breaking free from toxicity and reclaiming your peace. Your people are out there, ready to lift you up, hear you out, and help you boss up when you need it most. Remember, strength ain't just about muscles; it's about the love and support you surround yourself with. So, choose wisely, sis, because your circle can be your sanctuary when the storms of life start brewing.

Embrace Emotional Validation: Seeking *validation* isn't about being needy or insecure. No, it's about recognizing your feelings are real and valid, no matter what. Let your squad be the mirror that reflects back your truth, the cheerleaders in your corner reminding you that your emotions matter. Own your feels, queen, because you deserve to be seen and heard.

Grow Stronger With Each Connection: Every chat, every hug, every "I got you" from your inner circle adds another brick to your fortress of self-worth. Your support system ain't just about lending an ear; it's about lighting a fire within you, helping you rise from the ashes of what once held you down. Together, you are a force to be reckoned with—unstoppable, resilient, and thriving.

Chapter 6: Knowledge as Power: Educating Yourself on Emotional Abuse

The morning sun barely crept through the shades of Jenna's apartment, casting a pattern on the wall that felt like a metaphor for the shadow and light battle in her life these days. She perched on the edge of the worn-out couch, a cup of lukewarm coffee resting in her hands that had long lost their morning heat. The apartment was silent, save for the occasional hum of the refrigerator, which seemed to be protesting about its continuous labor more than usual.

Jenna had been turning a thought over and over in her mind, like a stone being polished by relentless waves, each cycle smoothing a rough edge. She had spent the last five years of her life with Marcus, her laugh catching partner, whose smile could light up a room but seemed to have a dimmer switch when they were alone. Slow realizations dawned on her that the sarcasm which once brought bursts of laughter now cut a little too deep, the teasing turned too personal, and his "just kidding" grew into a thick veil covering barbs.

She remembered the last big fight, where words flew like arrows, her defensiveness a pitiful shield. Later, she'd found solace on her best friend Tamara's porch, the wooden floorboards creaking in sympathy beneath her tired frame. "Girl, you know that ain't love," Tamara had said, her voice thick with concern, "Love don't keep score. Love don't tear down. Remember that." Jenna admired the strength Tamara always seemed to possess in spades.

The digital clock on the microwave blinked 8:47 AM – a reminder that the world outside was moving, indifferent to her turmoil. Jenna stood up, her movements pushing past the inertia of heavy thoughts. She needed to clear her head. Stepping out, she walked amidst the small homes lined up with precision on her block, the kind where everyone knew your name and business without you ever having to say a word.

Amid the hello nods from neighbors performing their own morning rituals, she pondered over the patterns that she now recognized as toxic. Games masked as affection, love withheld as punishment, a cycle that churned and repeated itself. The realization was bitter, the coffee's aftertaste a matching flavor to her sentiments. The courage to admit to oneself that love has been a masquerade is a solitary kind of bravery.

As she walked by Mrs. Hattie's front garden, the elderly lady called out, "You gotta weed the garden, baby, or the blossoms have no room to grow!" Jenna smiled at Mrs. Hattie's unintentional wisdom. Maybe it was time to pull out the weeds in her own life, even if it meant uprooting what she once nurtured with love and hope.

Turning back towards her home, Jenna murmured to herself, "Change ain't just coming, it's here." The road ahead wasn't merely a path of removal but a journey of replanting, where she could sow seeds of respect and watch them flourish in the soil of self-worth.

How many others out there were still under the spell of a love that hurt more than it healed?

Knowledge: Your First Step to Kicking Toxicity to the Curb

Let's keep it real—navigating the stormy waters of emotional abuse is no walk in the park. It's like trying to decipher a complex dance where the steps keep changing. But here's the kicker: **knowledge** about these toxic twirls and dips is your ticket to stopping the music and reclaiming your dance floor. In the grand ballroom of life, knowing the moves of emotional abuse and manipulation is powerful. It's like having the right shoes to glide across the floor confidently, avoiding those sneaky, stepped-on toes.

First things first, educating yourself on emotional abuse is akin to learning the dance vocabulary. Understanding gaslighting, manipulation, isolation, and verbal attacks is crucial. Imagine gaslighting as someone constantly changing the beat of the music, making you question your rhythm. Or manipulation as an unwelcome dance partner steering you away from the spotlight. Recognizing these signs and red flags is like knowing when to twirl away and when to make your grand exit.

But Honey, it doesn't stop at recognizing those toxic pirouettes. It's about understanding **why** some dancers stay on the floor, even when the tune turns sour. It involves diving deeper into the dynamics of toxic relationships and the emotional choreography that keeps individuals dancing in circles. Equip yourself with resources—books, articles, and those digital scrolls through websites that shed light on these shadowy patterns. And when the going gets tough, reaching out to a professional, like a therapist or counselor who knows all the right moves, can help guide you back into the rhythm of self-care and empowerment.

Recognizing the Rhythm: Healthy vs. Toxic

Once you've familiarized yourself with the steps of emotional abuse, it's time to tune into your own relationships. Reflect on those past and present dances and identify the patterns—were they a harmonious waltz or a tumultuous tango? By comparing these interactions to what **healthy** relationships look like, you can start to separate the roses from the thorns. Remember, a dance based on respect, communication, and clear boundaries is one where both partners shine, not step on each other's toes.

This is where setting and enforcing your boundaries comes into play, like choosing the playlist for your life's soundtrack. And let's not forget the importance of those reality checks from your squad. Having those **<u>trusted</u>**, objective voices whispering (or sometimes shouting) from the sidelines can help confirm when it's time to change partners, or in some cases, take a solo spin on the dance floor. Now, when I say 'trusted voices', let's underline and bold that word, because it's crucial. Listen, we've all got those sideline commentators in our lives who, despite lacking both experience and insight, always seem eager to share their two cents. And let's be real, more often than not, their input is tinted with shades of envy or malice. So, when you're filtering through these opinions, make sure the advice you're taking to heart comes from those who genuinely have your best interests in mind. These voices should be rooted in truth and objectivity, not marred by selfish motives or personal agendas. Remember, in this dance of life, you need a chorus that sings in tune with your well-being, not one that's off-key with its own discordant notes.

Cutting the Music on Toxic Patterns

Now, here's where you put on your dancing shoes and step into your power. Overcoming those toxic patterns requires a mix of acknowledgment, self-reflection, and strategy. Start by owning your part in the dance—were there times you followed a harmful lead or ignored the signs to exit stage left? Digging into those underlying beliefs and insecurities can be like learning a new dance genre—it's uncomfortable at first, but mastering it can set you free.

Developing coping mechanisms and strategies is your choreography for a healthier future. Whether it's through therapy, self-help exercises, or simply practicing mindfulness, each step is a move toward a dance where you're no longer tripping over someone else's moves but following your own rhythm. Surrounding yourself with positive influences ensures that your dance floor is filled with those who cheer you on, not hold you back.

Remember, the path from recognizing the dynamics of emotional abuse to stepping into your power is not a straight line—it's a dance, filled with twists, turns, and the occasional dip. But with knowledge as your foundation, you're well on your way to reclaiming your stage and embracing your worth, beyond those toxic bonds. And let me tell you, watching you dance to your own beat, owning your story—that's a performance worth applauding.

Gain Insights into the Dynamics and Signs of Emotional Abuse and Manipulation

Now, let's face it, deciphering the dynamics and signs of emotional abuse and manipulation is kind of like knowing the difference between real gold and fool's gold. It shines, it catches the eye, but only with a closer look and a bit of knowledge can you tell what's what. Emotional abuse, unlike physical counterparts, leaves no visible scars. It operates in the shadows of manipulation, eroding self-esteem and independence with each passing moment.

The most dangerous thing about emotional abuse is its

subtlety. Like a slowly dripping faucet, it chips away at your soul drop by drop, until you find yourself in a pool of self-doubt. One sign you're knee-deep in manipulation is when your thoughts no longer feel like your own. Suddenly, you're second-guessing every decision, your worth, even your sanity. It's because emotional abusers wield gaslighting like a sword, slicing through your reality until you're leaning on them for the "truth".

It's also the isolation for me. Abusers craft the scene so meticulously, convincing you the world is against you and they are your only ally. Honey, know this: if someone is isolating you under the guise of "protection" or "love", that's a red flag wearing boots and doing the Electric Slide. Real love doesn't cage you; it gives you wings.

Now, let's talk about verbal jabs and backhanded compliments. "You're pretty for a big girl," or "You'd be nothing without me." These comments, they cut deeper than they seem, each designed to chip away at your self-esteem. It's like being pricked by a thorn every day; you might not notice the damage at first, but over time, the pain accumulates, leaving you wounded.

Understanding emotional abuse and manipulation is the first step to turning on the lights and seeing the roaches

for what they are.

A Guide to Empowerment: From Surviving to Thriving

Step 1: Educating Yourself on Emotional Abuse

Let's break it down. First up, get the 411 on all the forms emotional abuse can take - we're talking gaslighting, manipulation, isolation, you name it. Dip into the knowledge pool - books, articles, websites, they're all your friends here. And trust, it's like unlocking a new level when you recognize these signs playing out live. Knowing is half the battle.

Getting a therapist or counselor on your team can be a game-changer. It's like having your personal coach, someone in your corner who's rooting for YOU. They'll help you navigate through these murky waters, and trust, that clarity they bring is next-level.

Step 2: Differentiating Healthy and Toxic Behaviors

Now, let's keep it real—reflect on your past or current relations. Essence Festival with the good vibes? Or more of a Fyre Festival disaster? Identifying those toxic patterns is key. And here's the tea, you gotta know what healthy relationship behaviors look like. Open communication, respect, boundaries—it's like a rhythm, once you catch it, you can't stop moving to it.

Setting boundaries isn't just about saying no; it's about teaching others how to treat you. It's like Beyoncé walking into a room—confident and commanding respect. And honey, when you communicate your needs and expectations, it's pure magic.

Seeking out those who genuinely uplift you can nourish your soul in ways you can't imagine. It's like having a personal cheer squad dedicated solely to your growth.

Step 3: Addressing and Overcoming Toxic Patterns

Look, it's easy to play the blame game, but owning up to your role in unhealthy dynamics? That's where your power lies. It's about shining a light on those dark corners of your insecurities and saying, "Not today, Satan."

Find those coping mechanisms that work for you. Therapy, self-help books, yoga—whatever keeps your boat afloat, darling. And surrounding yourself with positivity? That's the cherry on top. It's like moving from a toxic wasteland to a lush, vibrant garden.

Can you imagine the freedom of finally shedding those

toxic patterns like last season's fashion?

"Knowledge as Power" Framework

Understanding Emotional Abuse and Manipulation

First off, let's dive deep into recognizing the plays from the playbook of emotional abuse and manipulation. Understanding the various forms—from gaslighting to verbal attacks—and their signs illuminates the paths these toxic behaviors tread in a relationship. It's about adding pieces to the puzzle until the picture of a healthier relationship starts to emerge.

Differentiating Healthy and Toxic Behaviors

Honey, knowing the difference between what's nurturing and what's draining in a relationship is like knowing your worth and adding tax. This step is about undressing the disguised behaviors that toxify relationships and wrapping our arms around what wholesome and uplifting connections look like.

Strategies for Addressing Toxic Patterns

Addressing the patterns head-on is where the rubber meets the road. It's about equipping yourself with the armor of assertiveness and the shield of effective communication. We're laying out strategies that transform confrontations into constructive dialogues, turning what was once a battlefield into a tableau of understanding and respect.

Seeking Professional Help and Support

Navigating the murky waters of emotional abuse can indeed feel like being adrift on the New Jersey Turnpike, with every exit sign blurred and confusing. This is where seeking professional help comes in – think of it as your trusty GPS, not just recalibrating but also illuminating the path back to a place of safety and clarity. Embracing this step underscores the vital role of therapists, support groups, and helplines. They're not just waypoints; they are beacons of hope and understanding in the tempest of your journey.

Think of therapists as seasoned navigators, skilled in charting courses through emotional squalls. They offer not just directions but also insights into the patterns of the fog you're wading through. Support groups, on the other hand, are like fellow travelers, each with their own map, but all headed towards the same destination of healing and wholeness. Their shared experiences and collective wisdom can be both comforting and enlightening, a reminder that you're not alone in this journey.

And let's not overlook the role of helplines – they're the lighthouses in your darkest nights. At moments when you feel lost in the abyss, a compassionate voice at the end of the line can be the guiding light you need to find your bearings again.

Remember, this journey of recovery is not a solo expedition. It's a voyage that often requires a crew of support. By anchoring yourself with the right help, you're setting sails towards calmer seas and brighter horizons. This step is not just about seeking assistance; it's about empowering yourself with the right tools and companions to navigate your way back to peace and self-discovery.

Healing and Recovery

The final destination on this journey is healing and recovery, where self-reflection blooms and self-care flourishes. It's where you pick up the pieces, not to restore what once was, but to create something even more beautiful. It's about watering the garden of your soul until it's lush with love, respect, and understanding.

By arming ourselves with knowledge, differentiating the healthy from the toxic, and developing strategies to nip toxicity in the bud, we reclaim our power and pen the narrative of our lives.

This journey isn't about getting back to where you were—it's about soaring to new heights you never imagined possible. So, tell me, **are you ready to embrace your worth and cultivate a life overflowing with love, respect, and empowerment?**

Ready to Take on the World

Girl, you have just equipped yourself with some serious knowledge on emotional abuse! *Educating yourself on the dynamics of toxic relationships and manipulation is the ultimate power move.* Recognizing the signs of emotional abuse, understanding the difference between healthy and toxic behaviors, and developing strategies to break free from toxic patterns are all crucial steps in reclaiming your worth.

Knowledge is Power, Sis

Knowledge isn't just power; it's your shield against toxicity. By diving deep into the nuances of emotional abuse, you've armed yourself with the wisdom needed to navigate the murky waters of toxic relationships. *Educating yourself is like putting on a suit of armor before heading into battle.* You're ready to face whatever comes your way with a newfound sense of clarity and understanding.

Embrace Your Wisdom

Feel that empowerment coursing through your veins? *That's the strength that comes from educating yourself.* By differentiating healthy from toxic behaviors and learning to address manipulative patterns, you're paving the way for a brighter, healthier future. It's like you've unlocked a secret code to safeguard your heart and mind from harmful influences.

Keep Shining Bright

Girl, don't dim your light for anyone. *You are a force to be reckoned with, armed with knowledge and determination.* Stand tall, hold your head high, and never forget that you deserve nothing less than love, respect, and happiness in your relationships. You've taken the first step towards freedom—keep strutting down that path with unwavering confidence.

Stay True to Your Worth

As we close this chapter, remember this: *You are worthy of love that uplifts, of respect that honors your spirit, and of happiness that knows no bounds.* Educating yourself on emotional abuse is just the beginning of your journey to reclaiming your power. Stay strong, stay vigilant, and never settle for anything less than the love and respect you deserve. The world is yours for the taking, sis—go out and conquer it!

Chapter 7: The Mirror of Self-Reflection: Understanding Your Deservedness

The early morning sun threw a warm golden blanket over the streets, and the scent of fresh-brewed coffee mingled with the sound of the city waking up. Jasmine sat in the pocket of her small but cozy kitchen, stirring her cup with a slow, almost reluctant motion. Her mind, a carousel of thoughts whirl around past loves and murky waters of self-worth. She laughed to herself, a short, sharp sound that didn't quite reach her eyes, for she had once again let down her guard, and her heart, to Jamal.

She thought about her grandma's words, "Honey, you've got to stop watering dead plants," and she could almost feel the weight of her knowing look, the same look that seemed to push her to question her relationship choices. The mug she held was a chipped token from her last anniversary with him, a reminder of a sweet moment that soured faster than forgotten milk on a sunny day.

Just then, a draught slipped through the cracked-open window, carrying with it the laughter of children on their way to school. It reminded Jasmine of her simpler times, times when her biggest worry was whether her double Dutch skills would impress her friends. "Look at you now, girl, tangled in emotions more complicated than any jump rope routine," she muttered to herself.

She needed that childhood fearlessness, that untainted self-awareness. She had lost herself in cycles, toxic ones, that promised change but only dressed up the same disappointments in new clothes. Jasmine sipped her coffee, the bitter taste grounding her spinning thoughts. "Enough, Jasmine. You've got to see your own worth," she preached to her reflection in the mirror across from her.

Her phone buzzed on the counter, light glinting off its screen, an ominous beacon calling her to walk the plank once again. Jamal's name flashed, messages unread, but the sinking feeling in her chest read them clear as day. She wanted to set healthy expectations, to break the cycle of answering his siren call. Taking a deep breath, she could almost smell the change in the air, the sweet scent of empowerment mixing with her resolve. Would today be the day she finally chose herself over the comfort of the known, the day she found the strength to tell Jamal and her past self, "We deserve better"?

Let's Talk Worth: What You Really Deserve

Embarking on the journey of self-worth is like stepping into a room full of mirrors – each one reflecting a different aspect of who you are and what you truly deserve. Today, let's leave behind those toxic patterns like unwelcome guests at a party. We're not just brushing them aside; we're actively replacing them with empowering truths. It's time for a deep dive into the essence of your being, a heart-to-heart with the very core of your soul. This isn't about surface-level reflections; it's about peeling back layers to reveal your true beliefs, values, and the standards you should hold for your relationships. Think of this as your personal revolution, a transformative process that will redefine how you view yourself and what you accept from others.

Cultivating self-awareness is our secret weapon against the cycle of toxicity. It's about spotting those red flags from a mile away and saying, "Not today, chaos." It's understanding that the drama doesn't define you and that you're the scriptwriter of your own life. This journey of self-discovery isn't just about breaking free from what's holding you back; it's about rebuilding, with a foundation so strong that nothing less than respect, love, and genuine connection can make its way through your door.

Setting healthy expectations for relationships is like setting the bar high at a limbo contest - only the best will make it through. It's understanding that you're deserving of a relationship that mirrors your own worth, one that uplifts and empowers you. No more settling for less because, honey, you're aiming for the stars.

Let's keep it real; this journey of introspection isn't a walk in the park. It's akin to sorting through a closet that hasn't been touched since high school - daunting yet liberating. But, as they say, "The struggle is real, but so is the triumph." By diving into the depths of self-reflection, you're not just identifying those toxic cycles; you're actively breaking them.

Think of it this way: every time you engage in a moment of introspection, you're taking a step towards freedom. You're crafting a space where your worth is non-negotiable, where your values stand tall, and where your beliefs serve as the compass guiding you to healthier relationships.

Nobody said escaping to freedom was going to be easy, but darling, it's worth it. Just like that perfectly brewed cup of coffee, finding and embracing your worth is a process that demands patience, persistence, and a whole lot of self-love. So, let's lace up those sneakers, step up to that mirror of self-reflection, and prepare to meet the most refined version of ourselves. Here's to breaking free from those toxic bonds, one introspective moment at a time.

When you sit down with yourself, alone, cup of coffee in hand, watching the sunrise from your kitchen window, there's a quiet world waiting for you. It's the world of introspection; a sacred space where you meet your true self, away from the chaos, away from judgments. This is where you start. Taking time for introspection allows you to dive deep into your personal beliefs, values, and the standards you've unconsciously set for your relationships. It's like decluttering your grandma's attic; you might find treasures amidst things you no longer need.

Picture your mind as a garden. Over the years, it has been seeded with beliefs and values from experiences, people, and the culture around you. Some of these seeds blossom into beautiful flowers that represent the parts of yourself you're proud of—your kindness, your resilience. Others might grow into weeds, beliefs that suffocate your true self, telling you you're not enough or undeserving of happiness. Engaging in introspective practices is akin to tending to this garden, deciding which plants to nurture and which weeds to pull.

Engaging in introspective practices isn't about finding fault within yourself; it's about illumination and clarity. It gives you a flashlight in a room that's been dim for too long, allowing you to see clearly what your core values and beliefs are and how they align with what you truly deserve. Take meditation, journaling, or even long walks through the park. Each is a pathway to dialogue with yourself, a conversation that's long overdue. You might discover your belief in loyalty has made you tolerate mistreatment for fear of abandonment, or that your value of compassion has been twisted into self-sacrifice.

Now, armed with clarity about what truly matters to you, it's time to sketch the blueprint for your relationship standards. This isn't about crafting a wish list of ideal partner traits; it's about defining how you want to feel in a relationship, what boundaries are non-negotiable, and what values must be shared. It's asserting that respect, honesty, and support are not bonuses but basics.

Engaging in introspective practices lights the path to discovering your personal beliefs, values, and standards, guiding you toward what you truly deserve in a relationship.

Cultivating self-awareness is like becoming the detective of your own life. You begin to notice patterns, like how you always end up in the role of the caretaker or fall for the same type of emotionally unavailable partner. It's not about self-blame but recognizing the map you've been using and deciding it's time for a new one. Acknowledge the cycles; it's the first step in disrupting them.

With self-awareness, think of yourself as a protagonist in a story that's had too many repeat chapters. You know, the ones where you find yourself saying, "Why does this always happen to me?" Well, darling, it's because the script needs a rewrite. It's not just about knowing your lines but understanding why you choose to say them. Recognizing these patterns is empowering—it means you're no longer a bystander in your own life but the author of your new narrative.

Now, let's tie a bit of humor into this, shall we? Imagine toxic cycles as that annoying ex who keeps showing up at your family barbecues uninvited. At first, you might tolerate it because, hey, it's a small town, and folks talk. But eventually, you realize it's affecting your ability to enjoy your own party. Cultivating self-awareness is like finally deciding to tell them, "This is my space, you need to leave." It's about reclaiming your environment and your emotional well-being.

This is where we rise up. Break the cycle by setting clear, actionable goals for personal growth. Whether it's committing to weekly therapy sessions, setting boundaries in relationships, or dedicating time to self-care, these are actionable steps that signal to yourself (and the universe) that you're ready for change. Think of it as upgrading your internal operating system to better protect against future intrusions.

But here's the kicker: awareness without action is like having a map but not driving the car. It's fantastic to recognize where you are and where you want to go, but the journey requires you to put those keys in the ignition and start moving. It's about taking those insights you've gathered from your introspective deep dive and making tangible changes in your life.

What if recognizing your patterns is the key to unlocking a life where you're not just surviving, but thriving?

Setting healthy expectations for relationships starts with acknowledging your worth. Pretend you're shopping for a house. You wouldn't settle for one with a crumbling foundation just because it's available or because the previous one was worse, right? Similarly, understanding your personal worth allows you to set the bar for what you accept in relationships. You deserve a home that's secure, that shelters and nurtures you—a relationship built on respect, love, and mutual growth.

Let's get into the nitty-gritty. Healthy expectations are not about perfection but about respect, communication, and partnership. They're like the guardrails on a highway, designed to keep you safe and on track toward your destination. Setting these expectations is an act of self-love. It says, "I value my happiness and well-being enough to require that my relationships support it."

Incorporating your newfound understanding into your relationship dynamics can feel like planting a new garden. You're selecting seeds based on the lessons learned from introspection, the self-awareness gained, and the type of love you know you deserve. This garden is for plants that thrive on sunlight and honesty, watered with communication and mutual respect, where trust flowers freely. It's a beautiful, ongoing process of cultivation and growth.

Remember, it's perfectly okay to adjust these expectations as you evolve. What matters is that they always align with your understanding of your worth and the kind of love that nourishes your soul. This is not a one-size-fits-all deal; it's about what fits you, your values, and your aspirations. Be patient with yourself as you navigate this. Like any worthwhile endeavor, it takes time, effort, and a whole lot of self-love.

Engaging in introspective practices, cultivating self-awareness to disrupt toxic cycles, and setting healthy expectations based on a newfound understanding of personal worth are the pillars supporting your journey towards embracing what you truly deserve in a relationship.

You've embarked on a journey of deep self-reflection, sis. Through introspection, you've dug deep and uncovered layers of beliefs, values, and boundaries that shape your sense of worth. **Recognize the power in knowing what you deserve, queen —it's a game-changer.** By cultivating self-awareness, you're not just breaking toxic cycles, you're shattering them into a million pieces. **Now it's time to set the bar high in relationships, based on your newfound understanding of your own worth.**

Listen, as you move forward, remember that healthy expectations aren't just for show. They're your compass guiding you towards relationships that honor your true self. Gone are the days of settling for less than you deserve! It's time to thrive in bonds that uplift and cherish you.

So, as you take this wisdom with you, remember: you are worthy of love, respect, and joy. Let your newfound self-awareness and standards light the path to relationships that fuel your soul. *Keep slaying, keep growing, and above all, keep honoring the queen within you.*

Chapter 8: Voices of Resilience: Learning from Shared Stories of Survival

As sunlight brushed against the worn-out drapes of her modest home, Jasmine sat at the edge of the couch, hands clasped as if they alone could hold together the breaking seams of her heart. Leaves whispered secrets outside her window, affirming a simple truth she had long tried to mute—she was not alone in her struggle. She thought of the many other souls that had weathered the storm of toxicity, their survival tales a quilt of comfort she yearned to wrap herself in.

She caught her reflection in the glass of the clock hanging askew on the living room wall, its rhythmic ticking a reminder of time's indifference. Her thoughts drifted to the time when her laughter was a common melody in the house, before it turned into a somber echo of what once was.

Remembering the stories of others gave Jasmine a flicker of hope within the dim room. Those voices, like her own, had once trembled with doubt, yet sang of victory now. The musky scent of old books from the nearby shelf filled the room as if affirming that stories—their lessons and legacies—were timeless travelers. Visions of future gatherings where her own story might stitch up battered hearts brought a ghost of a smile to her face.

An uninvited puff of breeze fluttered through a small gap in the window, carrying the scent of fried chicken from the kitchen, and for a moment, Jasmine lost herself in a Sunday memory, where food was love, and silence wasn't heavy with words left unspoken.

She rose, straightened her spine like the oak tree that watched over her bedroom window, and moved to the kitchen, the wooden floor cold beneath her bare feet. As she stirred the greens in the pot, each swirl seemed to blend her fears with strength. She allowed her mind to wander to the thought of sharing her story one day, to sit among sisters and brothers, heads nodding in recognition as they shared the taste of shared triumph.

In the warmth of the kitchen, the fragrant steam rose like

spirits of comfort. Jasmine closed her eyes and whispered thanks to those spirits that danced in her midst—the ones that sustained her with their stories when she could barely sustain herself. She wondered who might be out there, simmering in silence, needing to hear her victories and setbacks, craving the seasoning of solidarity on their own journey of healing.

Who else is in their kitchen right now, stirring their own pot of hope, on the brink of finding the strength to share?

The Power of "Me Too": When Shared Stories Light the Path

Let's keep it real – leaving a toxic relationship is no walk in the park. It's more like navigating a dark, unmarked alley with no clear exit sign. But honey, here's something I've learned: you're not walking that alley alone. There's power, honey, immense power, in hearing "me too" from someone who's walked that same path and made it out into the sunshine.

Discover comfort and solidarity in the experiences of others who have overcome toxic relationships. Now, I'm not saying it's easy to open up about the struggles and wounds from a toxic relationship. It takes guts and a whole lot of trust. But the moment you do, you realize you're part of a resilient community. A simple "me too" from someone who's been there can act like a warm hug on a cold night. It's not just about comfort – it's knowing your fight is understood and shared. That's when healing starts, and let me tell you, it's beautiful.

When we talk about drawing strength from survival stories, it's not just about the happy endings. It's about the gritty battles fought, the moments of despair, and the flickers of hope that kept the fire burning. **Using survival stories as a source of hope and encouragement** teaches us that our past does not define our future. Each story is a beacon, guiding us through our own darkness. And believe me, seeing someone who faced similar battles come out on the other side with their head held high? It's like that first breath of fresh air after finally stepping out of that alley.

Sharing personal stories has a kind of magic to it, too. **Reflect on and share personal stories of overcoming toxicity as a means of healing and helping others.** It's like when you're at that family BBQ in the south, swapping stories and passing down wisdom. Except these stories can light the way for someone else caught in the shadows. It's saying, "If I made it, so can you," without actually saying it. It turns pain into purpose, suffering into hope.

Now, hold on. I'm not suggesting you grab a megaphone and broadcast your business to everyone who'll listen. This is about sharing within a space that feels safe and supportive. Maybe it's a one-on-one with someone who's just starting their journey out of toxicity, or perhaps it's a more organized setting, like a support group. The 'where' doesn't matter as much as the 'why'—and the why is about lifting each other up.

Stories have a knack for weaving us together, creating a tapestry of resilience that's much stronger than any one thread alone. When you share your story, you're not just unburdening yourself; you're adding your strength to the collective. It's a powerful reminder that we're not just survivors; we're thrivers. We don't just make it through; we come out with wisdom, strength, and a heart ready to help the next one in line.

So, let's embrace the power of shared survival stories. Let them be your guide, your comfort, and your inspiration. Because when we share, we find not only healing but a renewed sense of purpose and connection. And that, my friends, is where true freedom begins – freedom from the past, freedom to embrace our worth, and freedom to live a life beyond toxic bonds.

Remember, it's not just about escaping; it's about thriving on the other side. And with a little help from our shared stories, thriving is exactly what we'll do.

Discover Comfort and Solidarity in the Experiences of Others

You ever sit down at a family gathering and listen to the elders share tales of their challenges and how they pushed through? There's warmth and inspiration in those stories, kind of like when we hear about someone clawing their way out of a toxic relationship. It ain't just about the escape; it's about knowing you ain't alone in your struggle. That's where the comfort kicks in. It's about understanding that others have walked a similar rough path and made it to the other side where the sun shines a bit brighter.

Imagine a quilt made of different fabrics, each piece representing a story of survival from a toxic bond. As these pieces come together, they form something larger than themselves—a source of warmth and protection. This quilt doesn't just keep us warm; it wraps us in the collective strength and resilience of those who have gone before us. Their experiences, stitched together with threads of courage, create a tangible representation of solidarity and survival. It's a reminder that though the fabric of our stories may be unique, the strength we derive from them is shared.

Now, let me hit you with some facts. Research shows that sharing personal experiences with others who've faced similar challenges can significantly reduce feelings of isolation. It works like magic. Hearing that someone else has walked in shoes similar to ours and came out the other end can light a spark of hope in our own situation. It's that "if they can do it, so can I" vibe that gets us moving.

Sometimes, folks might feel like they're shouting into a void or that nobody really gets what they're going through. But when they hear stories of resilience and survival, it's like finding your people. It's a powerful reminder that you're not just a solitary tree bracing against the wind; you belong to a forest of survivors. And within this forest, there's a shared strength, a collective resilience that whispers, "We got you."

Discovering comfort and solidarity in the journeys of others offers a beacon of hope and a sense of belonging in our fight against toxicity.

Use Survival Stories as a Source of Hope and Encouragement

You know how sometimes a simple "You got this" from a friend can give you that push to face another day? That's the power of encouragement, and when it comes from someone who's been through the fire and came out with their spirit intact, it hits different. Survival stories are not just tales; they're lived experiences, beacons of light guiding us through our darkest times. They whisper to us, "If I made it through, honey, so can you."

Think of each survival story as a lighthouse standing tall amidst stormy seas. For those of us caught in the tumultuous waves of a toxic relationship, seeing that lighthouse can mean the difference between sinking and finding our way to safer shores. It serves as a reminder that storms do pass, and calm waters are within reach, as long as we keep swimming.

When we listen to the survival tales of those who've managed to escape the grip of a toxic relationship, it's like they're passing the baton of hope to us. It's a potent thing, hope. It's the spark that can ignite the fire within us, driving us towards liberation and healing. It reassures us that pain is not permanent and that the catastrophe we're currently facing has an end point.

Now, let's talk dynamics. It's easy to feel stuck in a loop of despair when you're dealing with toxicity. Survival stories disrupt this loop, inserting narratives of hope and resilience that challenge our current reality. They act as evidence that change is possible, and that with persistence, we too can alter the course of our lives.

In the end, it's not just about escaping; it's about thriving beyond the confines of what once held us back. Each story shared is a thread in the larger tapestry of human resilience, a collective narrative that speaks to our ability to overcome, adapt, and flourish even in the face of adversity.

Can finding comfort in these shared stories be the key to unlocking your own path to freedom?

Reflect on and Share Personal Stories of Overcoming Toxicity

Now, let me introduce you to a little framework I like to call "Voices of Resilience". This ain't just about talking; it's about transforming pain into power, and silence into strength. It's about sharing our tales, not just to unburden our hearts, but to light the way for others still fighting their battles in the dark.

Voices of Resilience

Overcoming Relationship Challenges

The first story in our framework highlights the journey from recognizing to reclaiming oneself from the clutches of a toxic relationship. It's about that turning point when the fog clears, and you see the relationship for what it truly is—a barrier to your growth. Recognizing toxicity is like finally noticing the warning signs on a hazardous road you've been traveling too long. This story celebrates the courage it takes to step off that hazardous path and pave a new one towards self-discovery and freedom.

Finding Self-Worth and Empowerment

Imagine being in a maze where every turn you take seems to lead you deeper into confusion—this is how being stuck in a toxic relationship can feel. The second story in our Voices of Resilience framework is about finding that hidden exit, the one that leads to rediscovery and empowerment. It's about transforming the narrative from being a victim to being the hero of your own story. This journey of self-worth often starts with a whisper, a quiet voice within that says, "I am more than this situation."

Thriving After Toxicity

The final story is about what happens after you escape the maze—when you not only find your footing but start sprinting towards a life you once thought was out of reach. It's about thriving, not in spite of the past, but because of the strength and wisdom gained from it. This story celebrates the blooming that follows the harsh winter, showcasing personal growth and the joy of rediscovering life's possibilities freed from toxicity's grip.

Collectively, these stories are more than just narratives; they're lifelines thrown into the turbulent seas of toxic relationships. They reassure us that while the journey may be fraught with challenges, it is also paved with resilience, growth, and the promise of a brighter tomorrow.

These components—the recognition of toxicity, the quest for self-worth, and the thriving beyond—interact and build upon each other. It's a cycle of healing that reinforces the idea that we are not defined by our circumstances but by our responses to them. The dynamics of this model underscore that healing is not linear; it's a spectrum that encompasses setbacks and victories, reflective of real-life experiences.

Through reflecting on and sharing our personal stories, we not only heal ourselves but extend a hand to those still navigating their paths out of toxicity. This interconnectedness, born from sharing and listening, fosters a community of resilience and strength.

As we wrap up this chapter, remember the power of solidarity and shared experiences in navigating toxic relationships. *Connecting with others who have walked a similar path can be incredibly validating, offering comfort and a sense of belonging that is truly priceless*. Lean on these survivor stories for hope and encouragement when your well runs low. *Let their victories light a fire within you, reminding you that you too can emerge from the darkness, stronger and wiser than before.* Take a moment to reflect on your own journey, and don't shy away from sharing your triumphs and challenges with others. *Your story has the ability to heal and inspire, serving as a beacon of hope for those still fighting their battles.* Together, we can rise above toxicity, reclaim our worth, and bask in the sunlight of freedom and self-love. *Stay strong, sis, the best is yet to come.*

Chapter 9: Nurturing the Self: Practices for Rebuilding Self-Worth

Michelle stared blankly at the steaming mug of chamomile tea cradled between her palms, feeling the warmth seep into her skin. The little kitchen, normally echoing with the sounds of laughter and the sizzle of something frying, lay silent except for the occasional whistle of the wind outside the window. Her thoughts swirled like the leaves in her cup, a stormy brew of past heartaches and the pressing need to heal.

She inhaled deeply, the floral scent wrapping around her, offering a temporary escape. Outside was awash with the colors of twilight, and children's distant laughter slipped through the cracks of the opening door as her niece burst in, small hands clutching a crayon masterpiece.

"Auntie 'Chelle, you gotta see this!" the little one exclaimed, oblivious to the tumult inside Michelle's chest. Her eyes, normally so quick to light up, took a second longer to respond, to see the whirls of purple and pink on the page.

"This is beautiful, baby girl," Michelle said, her voice steady, a direct contradiction to her inner chaos. A nod to self-care echoed through her mind as her phone buzzed with a reminder from her wellness app: "Time for your evening journaling." Journaling, that was something she could get behind, a bridge back to the self she'd lost in someone else's shadow.

Her thoughts returned to the art studio flyer she'd picked up earlier that day; painting had always ignited a fire in her, warming her from the inside out. Could she dare to reconnect with that part of herself again?

Pushing back from the kitchen table, she stood up and the floor creaked under the weight of her decision. Her muscles stretched, and she laughed softly to herself. "Girl, you gonna do this," she muttered, her words filled with a mix of uncertainty and excitement. "You gonna pick up that brush like you used to dream about in high school before life got all crazy."

She took a step, could almost hear the bristles scratching against the canvas, see the colors blending into an image of what used to be her passion. In her mind's eye, she was in that studio, lost in a moment of creation, her heart pulsing to the rhythm of her strokes. Her phone's reminder blinked once more: "Gratitude list before bed." She'd add that to her routine, another stitch in the patchwork of her self-esteem.

With each thought, with each small action, she felt the familiar weight of resilience gracing her shoulders. Power and possibility seemed to mingle in the evening air, seeping through the walls of her apartment.

Stepping out to the porch, she watched the stars emerge, one by one, like shy children peeking from behind the curtain of the night. As a gentle breeze stirred the loose tendrils of her hair, Michelle considered the journey she was embarking on. It might just be the path to rediscovering the woman who danced in her own light, untouched by the tarnish of another's disregard.

The neighborhood was quieting down now, curtain lights flicked out one by one, and Michelle's heart beat a soft, steady rhythm, in tune with the pulse of the city at dusk. She thought of the coming days, of the brushes and canvases that awaited, of the journal that would soon bear witness to her rebirth.

"Is it ever too late," she whispered to the night, "to paint a new beginning?"

Let's Get Real: Rebuilding the Temple within You

Let me tell you something, embarking on a journey to rediscover and nurture your self-worth after leaving a toxic relationship isn't just a walk in the park—it's like gearing up for Carnival after months of solitude. You're about to step into a realm filled with joy, self-discovery, and a whole lot of self-love, and trust me, it's worth every step.

The heart of our exploration in this chapter is about practicing self-care—not just those bubble baths and face masks (though they have their place), but engaging in activities that feed your soul, mend your heart, and strengthen your body. It's about embracing those practices that make you feel like you're taking a long, deep breath of fresh air after being cooped up inside. We'll dive deep into how mindfulness practices, hobbies, exercise, and yes, seeking therapy, are not just acts of self-love, but radical acts of reclaiming your worth.

Self-care isn't a one-time deal; it's a lifestyle, a conscious choice to prioritize yourself daily. It's about tuning into your own needs and allowing yourself the grace to meet them.

Think of it like planting a garden in your soul; it requires consistent care, the right environment, and a whole lot of love to flourish.

Engaging in **self-care activities** helps in reconnecting with yourself, rediscovering your interests, and, most importantly, rebuilding your sense of self-worth. It's the beacon that guides you through the fog, leading you back to a place where you can see your value, your strength, and your beauty, untainted by the toxicities of your past relationships.

Step by Step to Restoration: The TLC Your Soul's Been Craving

Step 1: Exploring Self-Care Activities

Start here: think of self-care activities that light up different corners of your mind, body, and soul. Whether it's doing yoga like you're trying to find your inner peace or dancing in your living room like nobody's watching, these activities should be all about bringing joy and relaxation into your life. Experiment and see what sticks; it's all about finding what makes your soul sing. And, honey, make it a priority, like making sure you never run out of your favorite coffee blend—non-negotiable.

Timeframe: Give yourself a month. Try different activities each week, and note how each makes you feel.

Step 2: Reconnecting with Personal Interests and Passions

Remember those painting classes you ditched or that guitar collecting dust in the corner? It's time to reconnect with those lost loves. Write down all the activities that used to bring you joy, choose one, and dive back in. Don't be shy to explore new territories, too. Ever thought of pottery or gardening? Now's the time! This is about rediscovering the joys that feed your soul and define you beyond anyone's shadow.

Timeframe: Spend a week making your list, then dedicate at least an hour each week to exploring these interests.

Step 3: Implementing Routines for Self-Esteem and Resilience

Building routines that boost your self-esteem and resilience is like laying down a solid foundation for your rebuilt temple. Incorporate daily affirmations—look in the mirror every morning and remind yourself of your worth. Practice gratitude; start or end your day by listing three things you're grateful for. Surround yourself with people who lift you up, not those who weigh you down. And remember, embracing your whole self, strengths, and flaws, is the real deal.

Timeframe: Start with daily affirmations and gratitude practice for a week and gradually introduce other routines.

Success looks like waking up feeling a bit lighter, a bit brighter, and a lot more like yourself. It's seeing the beauty in your journey, recognizing your worth, and embracing the freedom that comes with knowing you are more than enough, just as you are. Girl, you're not just surviving; you're thriving.

So, let's kick off those heels, roll up our sleeves, and get down to business. Rebuilding your self-worth is a journey worth taking, and baby, you've got the strength, the resilience, and the heart to make it happen. Let's do this, step by step, with all the love and care your beautiful soul deserves.

When it comes to bouncing back and rebuilding that self-worth, honey, self-care isn't just a nice-to-have; it's absolutely essential. Think about self-care as that hearty, nourishing soul food for your mind, body, and spirit. Just like mama's cooking can lift your spirits and bring comfort, self-care activities have that magical touch to foster mental, physical, and emotional well-being.

Let's get real for a moment. Life can be as unpredictable as Jersey weather—you step out into sunshine and suddenly find yourself caught in a downpour. Similarly, our mental and emotional states can flip without much warning. That's where self-care steps in, acting like that umbrella you stash in your bag. It's about having strategies in place to shield yourself from the rain, ensuring a bad day doesn't turn into a bad week. Whether it's journaling to clear your mind, yoga to ease your body, or meditation to soothe your soul, these practices help keep you grounded.

Now, envision your self-care routine as a custom mixtape filled with your favorite jams. Each activity, from mindfulness to hiking in nature, is like a track tailored to lift your mood and boost your spirit. You wouldn't listen to a song that brings you down, right? Same goes for self-care; pick the activities that resonate with you, making your heart sing and your soul dance. By doing so, you're not just going through the motions; you're actively participating in your healing journey, grooving towards a happier, healthier you.

Truth is, nurturing your well-being isn't a one-size-fits-all deal. It requires curiosity, a bit of experimentation, and plenty of self-love. It might mean saying 'no' to others so you can say 'yes' to yourself more often. Remember, this is about tuning into your needs and creating a self-care symphony that's uniquely yours. And just like finding the perfect rift in a song, when you hit that sweet spot of self-care, you'll feel it deep down.

In crafting and embracing a self-care routine that nourishes your mental, physical, and emotional well-being, you lay the foundation for rebuilding self-worth and stepping into your power.

Embrace Your Essence: A Guide to Rediscovering and Nurturing Your Passions

Reconnecting with your personal interests and passions is like dusting off an old photo album. Each page, filled with snapshots of your past joys and achievements, remind you of who you were before life got complicated. Over time, in the midst of navigating through toxic relationships and life's trials, you might've shelved this album on the highest shelf, forgetting its existence. But darling, it's time to bring it down, dust it off, and remember the vibrant, passionate individual you've always been.

Step 1: Exploring Self-Care Activities

First things first, let's carve out some 'me-time' to indulge in self-care activities that light you up inside. Kick it off by trying a bit of everything. Sign up for that yoga class at the Plainfield Performing Arts Center, grab a journal from the local bookstore, or take a mindful walk in Cedar Brook Park. You're curating a playlist of activities that resonate with your soul. Give it about a week for each to see what sticks.

Put those activities on repeat, scheduling them like they're hot dates you can't miss. Wednesday night? Oh, that's my dance class. Sunday morning? Time for that meditation session. These are the moments when you're prioritizing yourself, darling, no ifs, ands, or buts about it.

Step 2: Reconnecting with Personal Interests and Passions

Reflect on what used to make your heart skip a beat. Was it painting? Singing? Whatever it was, let's reintroduce it into your life. Start small; dedicate an hour or two a week to get back into it. It's like rekindling an old flame—awkward at first, but then all the good feelings start flooding back.

And don't be shy to flirt with some new hobbies. Always wanted to try pottery or learn to DJ? There's no time like the present to explore new horizons and discover hidden gems within yourself.

Step 3: Implementing Routines for Self-Esteem and Resilience

Craft routines that fortify your self-esteem and resilience.

Mornings could start with affirmations in the mirror: "I am strong, I am worthy, I am enough." Surround yourself with people who uplift you, whether it's family, old friends, or new acquaintances from your yoga class. Their encouragement is like sunshine for your growth.

Embrace all of you—flaws included. Love yourself through the missteps and learn from them. That's the real beauty of self-acceptance—it's acknowledging that you're a work in progress, and that's perfectly okay.

Could the key to unlocking your fullest potential lie in the passions and interests you've yet to explore or rediscover?

Tending to your self-esteem and resilience is akin to gardening. You've got to be patient, regularly nurture your garden, and not be afraid to pull out the weeds (aka negative self-talk). Plant seeds of positivity, water them with self-compassion, and give them plenty of sunlight by surrounding yourself with those who believe in you. Over time, you'll witness the blossoming of your self-assured, resilient self, ready to face life's challenges head-on.

Remember, self-esteem isn't an overnight bloom; it's cultivated through consistent care and compassion towards oneself. Integrate practices that reinforce your self-worth into your daily rituals. It could be as simple as jotting down three things you appreciate about yourself each night or setting boundaries that protect your peace and promote your well-being.

Building resilience is about recognizing your inner strength and ability to bounce back, much like the resilient nature of old trees in Sleepy Hollow that stand tall and strong, weathering storms and seasons. It's about knowing when to bend with the wind and when to stand firm. Incorporate activities that strengthen this resilience, be it through overcoming small challenges, fostering positive relationships, or practicing mindfulness to remain grounded in the face of adversity.

View your journey towards a positive self-image as an art project. There's no rush, no right or wrong way to do it, just your unique process of mixing colors, shapes, and textures until you craft a masterpiece that reflects your true essence. Learn to appreciate your progress, celebrate your victories, no matter how small, and remember that each step forward is a step towards the version of yourself you aspire to be.

By integrating self-care practices, reconnecting with your passions, and fostering routines that uphold self-esteem and resilience, you create a holistic approach to healing and personal growth, paving the

way for a reborn sense of self-worth and a brighter future.

Remember, sister-friend, tending to your own garden of self-worth ain't a one-time job; it's a commitment to your growth and happiness. Engaging in *self-care* ain't just about face masks and bubble baths (though those are essential too, honey). It's about nurturing your mind, body, and spirit like you're the precious gem you are. Prioritize activities that feed your soul, reignite your passions, and elevate your sense of self like the queen you are. So, whether it's meditating under the sun, indulging in your favorite hobby, or sweating it out in a Zumba class, make sure you're giving yourself the love and attention you deserve.

Reconnecting with what sets your soul on fire ain't just a luxury; it's a necessity for your well-being and growth. Your interests and passions ain't just hobbies; they're windows into your truest self. So, dust off that old paintbrush, pick up that forgotten novel, or lace up those dancing shoes, sis. Rediscover the magic within you and let your passions light up your path to healing and self-discovery.

Building a routine that uplifts and empowers you ain't just a suggestion; it's a game-changer in reclaiming

your worth and fostering resilience. Like a beautiful tapestry, weave together practices that boost your self-esteem, strengthen your spirit, and nurture a positive self-image. **Create a daily ritual that celebrates your unique essence and affirms the strength and beauty that reside within you.** So, rise and shine, queen, and seize each day as an opportunity to nurture, rediscover, and uplift yourself on this journey to freedom and self-worth.

Chapter 10: The Healing Journey: Embracing Patience and Self-Compassion

She stared at that old coffee stain on her wooden kitchen table, a fading remnant from a morning rush long past. The diffuse light of the morning trickled in through slightly parted curtains, casting an unsolicited spotlight on the rings of various sizes. They were like the marks of an old tree, each telling a story of haste, an argument, or a rare moment of morning tranquility.

The steam from her fresh cup rose in slow rebellion against the cool of the dawn air, curling into nothingness just as her thoughts tried to settle. But settling was a luxury she couldn't afford, not when her heart still rattled off in an arrhythmic beat, a hangover from the years spent in a love gone sour. She had let him go, or better yet, she had shrugged off the dead weight of his disdain. Still, love, even when it's toxic, leaves a shadow long after the light is turned off.

A pile of self-help books sat to her left, clean and uncreased. They promised a path to forgiving herself, to replace the doubt that sunk its claws in with every whispered memory. Self-compassion, now that's a road less traveled, she mused. She caught a glimpse of her own eyes in the reflection of the cold coffee pot, and the ghost of a smile played at the corners of her lips. Recognizing her strength took more effort than recounting her missteps, but she was learning to flip the script.

Her gaze turned out the window, where the world moved on as if nothing had happened. Children laughed on their way to school, car tires hummed on the damp streets, and there she sat, rooted in the transition between what was and what could be. The city continued its morning hustle, its beat vibrating through the window pane, a rhythm she'd move to, in time.

The phone buzzed on the table, a reminder of the day ahead. Work, perhaps a quick chat with her sister who had the humor of Queen Latifah and the wise vibes of Kerry Washington all rolled into one comforting voice. "Girl, you got this!" she'd say with a laugh, threading warmth into the fabric of her day. It rang true, each word a stepping stone away from the past and toward that which she dared to dream.

Her deep breaths drew in the scent of her brewed coffee and the faint smell of damp earth outside, new beginnings whispered on the wind. And just as the light shifted, so did her resolve.

What will it take, she wondered, for that first step to lead her down a road not marred by the shadows of old stains?

Honey, It's Time to Blossom

Girl, let me tell you, healing is not for the weak. It's like trying to walk in stilettos on a cobblestone street: challenging but, so worth it when you make it to the other side. In this chapter, we're going to dive deep into the heart of recovery, focusing on the gentle art of patience and self-compassion. Because, let's face it, after breaking free from a toxic relationship, the road to finding your fabulous self again can feel like you're in a maze blindfolded. But here's the thing—patience and self-compassion are the keys to unlocking a door to a brighter, more fulfilling future.

First thing's first: **accepting the healing process as an ongoing journey.** Picture this: you're in your home town, you've decided to take a scenic route home, but you find yourself lost. You could beat yourself up, or you could embrace the unexpected detour, discovering new parts of town you never knew existed. That's the essence of embracing the healing journey. It's not about racing to the finish line; it's about acknowledging that every step, no matter how small, is a victory.

Now, let's add a dollop of self-compassion to the mix. Imagine you're learning to make your grandma's famous sweet potato pie. The first try might be a disaster, but do you throw in the towel? No, honey, you give yourself grace, laugh it off, and try again. **Self-compassion is about treating yourself with the same kindness and understanding during your healing as you would while fumbling through that pie recipe.** Recognize your strength in facing your challenges head-on. Remember, you are not your past. You are a work in progress, and that's a beautiful thing.

It's also vital to shift your mindset towards the future. Consider it like spring cleaning; out with the old and in with the vibrant, joy-filled new. Drawing from the lessons of the past, we can cultivate a future-focused mindset, laying the foundation for a healthier, happier life. Imagine turning the lessons from those toxic bonds into empowering mantras. Yes, you went through that storm, but look at you—still standing, still shining.

Let's tie it all together, shall we? This journey we've been on together—from recognizing the signs of toxicity to reclaiming your worth—it's all been leading to this moment. The moment you realize your value doesn't decrease based on someone's inability to see your worth. The moment you start planting seeds for your garden of self-love to bloom.

You've got this. With patience, self-compassion, and a sprinkle of sass, there's nothing you can't overcome. You're not just surviving; you're thriving. So, as you turn each page of your journey, remember to embrace every moment with a heart full of grace and a soul fueled by resilience. Because, my dear, the world is waiting for your light to shine.

Healing is not a sprint; it's more like a cross-town journey, during rush hour—there will be stops, slow-downs, and sometimes you might feel like you're not moving at all. That's the very first thing you've got to understand. Healing from emotional abuse is not about crossing some finish line. It's about the everyday choices you make to treat yourself with kindness and patience.

If you're planting a garden in your backyard, you wouldn't just throw some seeds on the ground and expect a lush garden the next day, right? Healing is like tending to that garden. Each day, you might water it, remove a weed or two, or maybe just check on how it's doing. Over time, with care and attention, it starts to bloom. This analogy underscores that healing requires ongoing effort and patience. The progress might seem slow, but with each day you're moving toward a healthier you.

It's crucial to recognize that the path to healing isn't the same for everyone. Some folks might find themselves taking a few steps back after making significant progress—and that's perfectly okay. Healing isn't a linear process. It's filled with ups and downs, and that's something that's often overlooked. You might have days where the pain feels fresh, and others where you feel strong, resilient, and capable. Accepting this ebb and flow as part of the journey is crucial.

In the heart of Plainfield, just like in any community, we rally around those facing tough times, because we know that every journey is unique. Similarly, healing from emotional abuse requires a community—whether it's friends, family, or professionals—who acknowledge your progress, no matter how small, and support you through the setbacks. Their patience is a mirror of the patience you need for yourself.

And here's the thing, healing is intensely personal. Only you truly know the depth of your pain and the height of your barriers. That means, only you can pace your healing journey. There's no shame in taking your time. If you were learning a new dance, you wouldn't beat yourself up for not getting it right on the first try, right? Extend that same grace to yourself when navigating your healing process.

The key point is to acknowledge the healing process as an ongoing journey requiring time and patience.

Let's talk self-compassion. Now, this is a game-changer. Practicing self-compassion starts with recognizing and accepting your personal challenges and the progress you've made. It's like looking at yourself in the mirror and saying, "Girl, you're doing the best you can, and that's more than enough."

Self-compassion is realizing that healing from emotional abuse isn't a straight path—it's more like navigating the streets of the city with its one-ways and unexpected detours. But instead of getting frustrated with the detours, it's about embracing them, maybe even discovering something new and beautiful on a path you wouldn't have taken otherwise.

Think of it this way: when a friend is going through a tough time, what do you do? You listen, offer a shoulder to cry on, and remind them of their strength and resilience. Self-compassion is essentially doing that for yourself. It's being your own ride-or-die, your own cheerleader, and recognizing that the journey you're on is tough, but so are you.

Now, imagine you're wearing a backpack filled with bricks, each brick representing a hurtful moment or memory. Self-compassion is taking a moment, maybe sat on a bench in Cedar Brook Park, to take out each brick, acknowledge it, and then decide whether it's time to put it down. It's understanding that some days, that backpack might feel heavier, and that's okay. It's about being gentle with yourself in those moments.

One analogy that might hit home is thinking of self-compassion as applying a soothing balm to a burn. The healing won't happen overnight, but with each gentle application, the pain eases, the damage heals a bit more, and you're reminded of your own capacity to care for yourself.

So, if you were to approach every day with self-compassion, how might your journey to healing change?

Looking ahead is not just about setting goals or making plans—it's about cultivating a mindset that sees every experience, good or bad, as a step toward a future where you are healthier, happier, and fully in love with who you are.

It's about leveraging the lessons learned from past experiences to build a life that's not just about surviving, but thriving.

Consider this: every time you choose to practice patience and self-compassion on your healing journey, you're laying down a brick on the path to a brighter, more fulfilling future. It's not about forgetting the past or ignoring the pain; it's about transforming that pain into wisdom, strength, and resilience that guides you forward.

Imagine you're at a crossroad deciding which way to go. A future-focused mindset is like choosing the path that might be longer or more challenging but ultimately leads to a beautiful place you haven't seen yet. It's about making choices today that your future self will thank you for.

Much like preparing for a significant event —be it a community celebration or a personal achievement—cultivating a future-focused mindset requires intention, effort, and sometimes, a little creativity. It's about decorating your life with experiences, people, and practices that align with who you want to become, not just who you've been.

By acknowledging healing as a journey requiring patience, practicing self-compassion, and cultivating a

future-focused mindset, we equip ourselves with the tools needed for a fulfilling and healthier life ahead.

Embrace the Journey Towards Healing

Remember, darling, healing is a journey, not a sprint. It's a road with twists and turns, hills and valleys, but with each step, you grow stronger. **Patience is your faithful companion** on this path, reminding you that progress takes time and setbacks are just pit stops, not dead ends. Every day you choose yourself is a victory, a step closer to the light at the end of the tunnel.

Shower Yourself with Self-Compassion

It's time, honey, to be gentle with yourself. Embrace your flaws as part of your unique beauty, your scars as badges of survival. **Self-compassion is not a weakness; it's a superpower** that fuels your resilience. Your challenges don't define you; they refine you, shaping you into a bolder, braver version of yourself.

Look to the Bright, Beautiful Horizon

As you journey forward, keep your eyes on the prize: a life filled with love, joy, and fulfillment. Every tear shed in the past waters the seeds of your future happiness. **You've

learned, you've grown, and now it's time to soar. The person you're becoming beckons you with open arms to a future brighter than you ever imagined.

Reclaim Your Power, Crown Yourself Queen of Your Destiny

This journey, honey, is not just about leaving the past behind; it's about crafting a future that shines with your own radiant light. With each step you take, you reclaim your power, your worth, and your voice. **You are the author of your story, the architect of your dreams**. So stride forth, head held high, for your throne awaits—crown yourself queen of your destiny.

Epilogue

Finding Your Freedom and Embracing the Fabulous You

As we wrap up this empowering journey together, think of this conclusion not as an ending, but as a commencement speech at the start of the rest of your fabulous, freedom-filled life. Honey, you've been through the wringer, but you're standing here today, stronger, wiser, and more fabulous than ever. It's like stepping out into the refreshing air after being cooped up in a stuffy room for way too long. That's right, you've opened the windows to your soul, and it's time to let your spirit breathe.

You've waded through the murky waters of toxic relationships, armed with nothing but your resilience and the burning desire for something better. You've peeled back the layers of doubt, fear, and manipulation and emerged ready to bask in the warmth of your worth. It's been a journey from the depths of uncertainty to the peaks of self-reclamation, and honey, you've climbed that mountain in heels!

Remember the essential truths we've unpacked together: recognizing the red flags of emotional abuse, understanding the psychological chains that bind us to our tormentors, and the life-changing magic of saying "No more." We've navigated the tricky waters of leaving a toxic relationship and setting sail towards healthier horizons. It's like figuring out that the secret ingredient in your grandma's famous sweet potato pie was love all along – it changes everything.

Now, how do you put all this newfound wisdom to work in your life? First off, flex that self-love muscle daily. Whether it's setting boundaries like a boss, prioritizing your wellness, or simply taking a moment to breathe and appreciate the divine queen that you are, it all counts. Remember, it's the little acts of self-care that weave a protective tapestry around your heart.

And let's not forget the power of community. Sharing your story is not just cathartic; it creates ripples that can turn into waves of change for others. Whether in Jersey or anywhere else in the world, your voice can be a beacon for those still stumbling through the dark.

Of course, no book can cover every nook and cranny of human experience, and mine is no exception. The road to healing and self-discovery is as unique as a fingerprint – sometimes messy, often beautiful, but always yours to claim. So keep seeking, learning, and growing. The end of this book is simply the start of your next chapter.

Let me leave you with this, as you step boldly into your future: Embrace the journey with all its twists and turns. Love fiercely, not just others, but especially yourself. And never underestimate the power you hold within.

Remember, it's not just about escaping to freedom; it's about **thriving** on the other side. So go ahead, strut into your new life with all the grace and swagger of a runway model at New York Fashion Week. Because, darling, the world is your catwalk and it's your time to shine.

And as the phenomenal Maya Angelou once said,

"I can be changed by what happens to me. But I refuse to be reduced by it."

Carry those words in your heart as you conquer each day. With love, sass, and a sprinkle of audacity, there's nothing you can't achieve.

www.ingramcontent.com/pod-product-compliance
Lightning Source LLC
Chambersburg PA
CBHW051210120626
46547CB00013B/1287